7 HABITS *of*
Deeply Fulfilled Artists

Your Aesthetic Needs
& How to Meet Them

7 HABITS *of*
Deeply Fulfilled Artists

Your Aesthetic Needs
& How to Meet Them

Ellie Harold

Frankfort, MI

Anecdotes and examples used in this book represent actual events; however, some names have been changed to protect the privacy of the individuals involved.

Contact the author through her website:
www.EllieHarold.com.

Publisher's Cataloging-in-Publication Data

Harold, Ellie.
   Seven habits of deeply fulfilled artists : your aesthetic needs & how to meet them / Ellie Harold.
      p. cm.
   Includes bibliographical references.
   ISBN: 978-0-615-59647-1
   1. Artists—Psychology. 2. Creation (Literary, artistic, etc.)—Psychological aspects. 3. Self-actualization (Psychology).   I. Title.
N71 .H275 2012
701—dc23

                                                2012919067

Design: **Meredith McNabb, Sarah Swanson**
Cover Illustration: **"Bright Ideas" Ellie Harold, 30" x 30", oil/canvas, 2012**
Back Cover photo: **Linda LaViolette**

Printed in the United States of America on acid free paper.

To Roo

For continuing to encourage me to do the Art
that needs to be done by me.

*T*his is the true joy in life,
    the being used for a purpose recognized
    by yourself as a mighty one;
the being a force of nature instead of
a feverish, selfish little clod of ailments and
grievances complaining that the world will not
devote itself to making you happy.

I am of the opinion that my life belongs to the
whole community and as long as I live it is my
privilege to do for it whatever I can.

I want to be thoroughly used up when I die, for
the harder I work the more I live. I rejoice in life
for its own sake. Life is no "brief candle" to me.
It is a sort of splendid torch which I have got
hold of for the moment, and I want to make it
burn as brightly as possible before handing it on
to future generations.

George Bernard Shaw
Man & Superman
Dedicatory letter

CONTENTS

Introduction

Simply because you've opened this book, I'm willing to bet you're drawn to making some kind of art. It's not important if you realized this at age 5 when your kindergarten teacher put a paintbrush in your hand; or at 50 when you finally signed up for piano lessons; or at 70 when you wrote your first lines of poetry. No matter how old you now are, I believe there's a good chance that making art is a profound, even necessary way for you to make sense of your life and, the more you do, the more purposeful and fulfilled you feel.

If, however, you feel an attraction for making art and you don't do it, chances are equally good you feel discontented with your life, even when nothing seems particularly wrong. Not understanding your dissatisfaction, you may wonder why your friends seem content while you're not. Perhaps you've tried to do more of what they're doing: spend more time with your family, volunteer to do good works, redecorate your home or, if all else fails, go shopping or bake (and eat) cookies. You may notice, however, that the more these activities dominate your life, the less satisfied you become.

No matter what kind of worthy causes capture your time, if you're an artist and you're not making art, you will be more or less miserable. I've learned this both from my personal experience as a painter and writer, and from my professional experience of counseling and coaching, not to mention living with, frustrated artists. I've observed that when pursuing their artistic goals, artists rarely question the meaning of their lives. When suffering from what Eric Maisel calls the "van Gogh blues," however, they feel thwarted, blocked, and maybe even a bit crazy.

Why is this? I believe it's because artists differ from non-artists in one important way: An artist's sense of well-being depends upon meeting aesthetic or artistic needs. Whether she realizes it yet or not, art makes an artist's life worth living. If an artist fails to recognize this phenomenon, her needs are ignored or neglected and she feels unfulfilled.

It's simple. If you don't eat food when you're hungry, you don't feel good. In the short term, your stomach growls and you feel grumpy—this is your body's way of reminding you to give it some fuel; if you're deprived of food for a long time, you starve. The so-called starving artist, however, isn't hungry for a steak and salad, but is craving food for the soul.

Soul is a largely unknown but deeply felt aspect of our existence, one we perceive typically only in brief glimpses. A peak experience, a profound meditation or, for the artist, an art-making session, may awaken us to this sense that there's more to us than meets the eye. In "Song of the Open Road," Walt Whitman described his fleeting awareness of his soul: "I am larger, better than I thought," he wrote. "I did not know I held so much goodness." We feed our soul, or whole self, by giving attention to its evolving needs. If you're an artist with aesthetic needs and you don't give yourself the art experiences you crave, your soul has its ways of getting your attention: irritability, boredom, and depression, to name only a few.

Joseph Campbell explored at length how the soul-level of our existence uses myth to communicate both universal and personal wisdom. The most important of these spiritual truths, he concludes, is "follow your bliss:" The things in life that move us— for which we experience desire, attraction or hunger—are actually pulling us forward on a path of self-realization, which Campbell referred to as the hero's journey.

Motivational research psychologist Abraham Maslow provided a psychological framework for understanding Campbell's metaphorical journey. Maslow describes the challenge of self-realization in terms of a Hierarchy of Needs, from the most basic physical necessities to those required to fulfill our utmost human potential. Life, it seems, is always moving us toward that destiny. The ideas in this book, then, while of little or no interest to people who are not artists, serve as soul food to those living at the Aesthetic Need level of Maslow's Hierarchy.

While I'd been a student of Maslow's work for many years, I first stumbled upon the awareness of its application to artists in 2008. At that time I offered a workshop through a local art center in Norcross, Georgia entitled Goal-Setting for Artists: Taking Your Art to the Next Level. As an experienced public speaker and workshop facilitator, I was impressed with how the material about aesthetic needs grabbed the attention of the 30 participants. I noticed more than one person weeping as I presented each of the Seven Habits of Deeply Fulfilled Artists. However, it was the tearful woman who stood up at the end of the workshop who convinced me these good ideas could benefit a larger audience.

"You've given me my soul back!" she exclaimed. "I came here because I've been miserable. I'd convinced myself that since my work isn't selling, I should do something else. I was ready to quit. But I haven't been happy with that decision either. I've known that I *want* do art. But now I know I *need* to do art and I *must* do art."

In the many years of sharing similar ideas before a church congregation, I'd never before heard such stirring testimony. I felt my words had truly hit the mark. I know I didn't actually give that woman her soul back, but the ideas I'd shared seemed to help her reclaim for herself what she'd almost given away. Not only did she feel better, but I also felt particularly satisfied that I'd been able to alleviate the suffering of a fellow artist. Her experience also helped me affirm a refinement for my own career I was in the process of making: I was being called to work exclusively in service to art by doing my own artwork and helping other artists do theirs.

When I offered that first goal-setting workshop, the participants were mostly women[1] and a few men who painted or did some other form of 2-D visual art; however, there were also several writers, an actor and an opera singer. Some of the participants considered themselves to be professional artists, but most did their artwork on an occasional or part-time basis. Without exception, everyone present claimed there was a gap in the amount or kind of art they were producing and what they felt would be most satisfying.

Although the workshop was scheduled early in January, getting everyone revved up to make resolutions for a new art-production regime was not part of my aim. Instead, I wanted to offer simple organizing principles that would work over the long term. These had worked not only for me but also for those I'd counseled over many years and for friends who seemed to be satisfied in their art-making lives.

The Seven Habits of Deeply Fulfilled Artists describes attitudes and behaviors that channel an artist's natural inclination to evolve into practices that result in a productive and satisfying art life. There's nothing earth-shatteringly new here. But I'm told they have the effect of encouraging and inspiring artists to do what on some deep level they already know they must do—art!

I've written this book for both amateur and professional artists. While their circumstances may vary, all find themselves with the same soul hunger. The amateur category includes many who have come to art later in life. You often find amateurs of both genders, but mostly women, at community art centers or adult-ed classes. The older artist rarely considers art a vocation or profession. He's retired, or she's the middle-aged wife of an affluent professional. For the amateur, art is frequently viewed as an interest, a diversion or a

---

[1] For this reason I use the feminine pronoun almost exclusively in this book.

pastime. He doesn't paint, he "dabbles." She balks at calling herself an artist, explaining that she only "takes classes."

The older artist often thinks of herself (and is often treated by others) as a perpetual student or dilettante. She doesn't take her art-making seriously; consequently, neither does anyone else. Studio or practice time consists of whatever is left over after attending to everyone else's needs. Paintings, labored over for weeks or months, are left unsigned, given away as gifts, or hung in the local library with a $50 price tag. After all, painting is just a hobby, something for fun. If you don't do your hobby, who really cares?

Soul-killing issues plague working artists as well. The problem for professional artists isn't that they don't take their art seriously. Their desire is sincere yet they suffer for believing they lack the time, money and energy to make art after attending to other responsibilities. Or, they argue that although they're doing some kind of artwork, it's not the sort they want to do. Other full-time artists are just plain discouraged—their best efforts don't seem to connect with anyone and cynicism threatens to stop art-making altogether. It's the rare professional who doesn't periodically come up against one or more of these attitudinal obstacles.

Amateurs often don't admit to a need to make art, while working artists know they need to, but feel thwarted in their attempts to make the best art of which they are capable. None of this would be problematic, of course, if the person coming to art later in life could be simply be satisfied with a passing interest or dabbling. Or if the professional artist could be convinced that making a living doing anything art-related was enough. Unfortunately, the effect of such settling-for-less is that art-making has a tendency to slide to the back burner of the artist's life and sometimes off the stove altogether.

If the thought of never making art again makes you cringe, this book is for you. *Seven Habits of Deeply Fulfilled Artists* is designed to help you understand that your desire to make meaningful art is not a fanciful whim but a need. Based on the premise that a true artist, young or old, will never be satisfied by doing art in anything less than a committed fashion, this book will help you explore the meaning of art in your life. And, it will remind you to align yourself with actions that honor what really matters most.

Seven Habits of Deeply Fulfilled Artists is organized in several parts: "Soul Hunger," the first part, relates who we are to the needs it is most vital for us to fulfill. The second part offers "Soul Food," nourishing morsels for approaching the work of art in a congruent and satisfying way. The "Soul-Full" section concludes the book by painting a picture of life as a Deeply Fulfilled Artist.

My desire is that this book inspires you to deepen your love of your artistic purpose. This book doesn't promise you will never again be unhappy, but it does give you tools to address your discontent in constructive, art-related ways. I believe reading it will give you a deeper and perhaps more loving relationship with your life and art.

Dr. Richard Moss, one of my teachers, invites his students: "Let love win." We spend too much of our life struggling to be right, successful, attractive and competent and not enough time simply surrendering to the love we naturally have for the life we've been given to live. Letting love win means forgiving ourselves (and others) for falling short of our expectations and opening more completely to what we were created to be. For us as artists, when love wins, our love of art leads us toward bliss and fulfillment. Let us go now to that place.

Ellie Harold
Frankfort, MI
October 2012

Prologue

A (Not Entirely) Tragic
Tale of a Frustrated Artist

My grandmother, Ethel Downing Harold, considered herself an entitled member of the Southern aristocracy. When her only son, my father, was born in 1912, she declared her fine figure had been ruined. Not only that, but in her esteemed judgment, Charles Louis Harold, Jr. was apparently good for nothing—with one and only one exception—he could draw extremely well. His ability apparently balanced his flaws. So while grandma shipped daddy off to military boarding school in Virginia (where at 13 he procured bootlegged hooch and cigarettes for the other cadets), she also made sure he studied art in Paris when he was 20.

Returning home from Europe in time for the Great Depression, my father hired on with the Brooklyn Daily Eagle newspaper. Thus he began his career as a commercial artist by day and an entertaining boozehound by night. One thing led to another. Dad met mom, and more things led to other things, including a baby conceived out of wedlock and, after an unsuccessful attempt to take his own life, my mother became his wife and delivered four more children.

Back in the day before photographs were widely used in advertising, illustrators filled the pages of all the national magazines with their artwork. During the 40s and 50s my dad freelanced for Madison Avenue art agencies. He won a prestigious industry award for his rendering of van Leeuwenhoek for a Listerine ad that later turned up in one my high school science books. If you've seen the television series "Mad Men," you have a good idea of how his days at the office might have been spent.

Van Leeuwenhoek by C. L. Harold

One day in 1959, dad announced he'd taken a salaried job with Lockheed Aircraft. The family, now consisting of mom and the three kids who'd not yet left for college, packed up and moved to Marietta, Georgia. There, in one of the largest defense plants in the country, my father spent his days drawing military airplanes. The steady job was thought by many to be good for him and for the family. There was no liquor at work and, if his domestic drinking necessitated a sick day, he still got paid. When the enormous C-5A was being rolled out, he drew images of it fourteen hours a day because he didn't feel he could turn down the overtime pay. Then, when the C-5A was complete and in production, there were no more planes to draw and my father was laid off.

Lou, as his Lockheed cohorts called him, then spent a couple of years doing layout work for the local newspaper. As the printing process became more mechanized, however, this work dried up as well. There were a few jobs doing architectural renderings, and, then, after a humiliating stint as a security guard on night shift, retirement with a small pension.

I can count on one hand the times I saw my father do artwork for pleasure. Once, he made a pair of pen and ink street scenes, one of Paris, the other of Charleston, both cities he loved. He worked on a large drawing table set up on the dining porch, always on Watman board, always with about 20 small bottles of India ink on a small taboret, and an assortment of pens and fine sable brushes.

If I was quiet, he'd let me watch. The way he developed a painting always seemed like magic I couldn't get enough of, and, when he'd finished, I would secretly hope he'd give it to me. I didn't understand when one day I came home from school to find the Charleston painting with a huge black X painted across it. He'd worked on it for weeks and now it was ruined. He'd ruined it. I didn't understand.

My father also produced an occasional darkly humorous greeting card, which would be directed to his best friend, my uncle Freddy, or to my oldest sister, Beeby, for holidays or on the occasion of the birth of a child. The only one I ever received is the one reproduced here, sent to my first husband and me for Christmas, 1978, a few months after we'd moved to Montana.

This card speaks volumes about my dad. He hated Christmas—the expense, the mess, the way the tree interfered with the décor of the house—pretty much everything about it. Most years, he simply drank his way through the ordeal, using eggnog with Jack Daniels to conjure up the good cheer the rest of us (me) wanted so badly. What was he thinking, I wonder, as he sat in the more or less empty nest of my parents' home, creating this macabre holiday celebration scene? At the time I received it, it struck me he'd attained the pinnacle of perfectly executed black humor, worthy of *The New Yorker*. I loved it.

Let Us Give It a Whirl, C.L Harold, 1978

As it turned out, this was the last card my father ever created. His youngest child had recently turned 21 and he was rounding the corner toward 67—he'd done his duty as breadwinner for wife and children. In March 1979, after an argument with his 96-year-old mother, he drank half a bottle of vodka to wash down some Darvon capsules he'd hoarded from recent dental procedures

Depressing, huh? Of course it is! This is the story of the largely unfulfilled artist—the one who apparently missed the point of life: the one who didn't know how to appreciate the talent he'd been given; the one who was so miserable he made a point of making others miserable too. My father once joked about his domestic situation that he would willingly have traded his five children for two good basset hounds. For many years it was my conscious and unconscious desire to figure out how I could have made my father happy and thus prevented his suicide. Therapy helped me to understand, however, that I was not responsible for his tragic actions. And neither would basset hounds have done the trick.

All sorts of things can come out of tragedy and I vowed to find the good as well as the bad. Eventually, I learned how to respond creatively to the life of Charles Louis Harold; for once my father killed himself—a reaction to what I believe was at bottom a lack of perceived meaning—it became clear to me that I never would take my own life. Instead, my life would become not only a search for meaning, but also a celebration wherever it could be found. I've since discovered there's much to be gleaned in life, even from a legacy of dissatisfaction. I've been determined to get what I could, sooner rather than later, but better late than never.

When I was ten years old, I decided to enter a citywide art contest being held by a local civic group. I had a great idea to make a drawing of Kennesaw Mountain, a familiar landmark in a nearby national park. I imagined it clearly—an old mule-drawn cart and driver on a road leading to the mountain. I did the best I could with what I now know to have been an ambitious project and, when I believed it was finished, took the drawing to my father. He looked it over while I waited nervously for his judgment. It wasn't long in coming. He simply said, "The perspective's all wrong," and handed it back to me.

Devastated, I did not enter the drawing in the contest. In fact, I didn't draw again for twenty years. When I did, however, in a figure drawing class at the University of Montana, I received high marks for my work. I thought there must be some mistake, that the instructor was just being kind to me. But he wasn't. The A's were consistent. I was not half-bad; my drawings were actually good.

During that time I flirted with art: I taught myself to weave using wool I dyed by hand. I occasionally made sketches. After that, however, it took me another twenty years to begin a full-fledged art career.

As a result of all this life experience, I believe I have more than a few things to say about what it takes to overcome the obstacles to being the artist you are. I know the tragedy of the frustrated artist who was my father, and also the grace of finding fulfillment in the art I was meant to do.

PART ONE

SOUL HUNGER

Needs "R" Us

What you seek is seeking you.
~ **Rumi**

What do you want to be when you grow up? How many times did your well-meaning aunts and uncles ask you this? A harmless question, easy enough for a child, right? If only it were that simple. If only we could anticipate our future at a very young age.

It does happen occasionally, of course. Only yesterday I heard an interview on NPR with a ballerina who had known since she was 6 that she wanted to dance. More frequently, however, the answers our child-self gave those nosy adults had nothing to do with what we actually ended up doing.

Looking back, it may seem our choices were limited by educational opportunities, the economic climate, our family responsibilities and other extrinsic factors. In other words, by "life's many vicissitudes." (According to my Aunt Nornie these ups and downs formed "life's rich pageant" and, added "jewels to your crown in heaven.") In my own case, at least, the most limiting factor was my own ignorance—I didn't know enough about myself to be able to predict who or what I'd become.

In high school I imagined my adult life as a Ph.D. college professor, married with two kids. In 1970, however, when student strikes closed Boston University, I chose to go hitchhiking cross-country with a new boyfriend. When I returned, my parents kicked me out of the house. Instead of getting my education paid for by them, I had to support myself. By the time I made it back to school, I needed to be more practical about my career choice. I ended up becoming an R.N., then an ordained minister, and, eventually, an artist. I never got a bachelor's degree or had children and didn't commit to marriage until I was 45. Who could have known any of this in advance? Like many of my generation, I appeared to be drifting; I see now, however, I was simply gathering information.

A Hierarchy of Needs

Until we've had a good taste of life, we don't really know what we're suited for, what we're capable of, and what we want to do with our lives. The Big Questions, "Who am I? What am I here for? What should I do with my life?" really take a lifetime to answer. It's a tricky business, too, as what might have satisfied us at one stage of our life, no longer does. We don't stay the same. We are, as the Russian philosopher Gurdjieff stated, "self-evolving organisms."

How do we evolve? Psychologist Abraham Maslow theorized that we're motivated to develop as we learn to fulfill a series of hierarchical needs. Only as we've met our needs at each successive level do we become aware of the needs at the next level. When each level of need has been adequately addressed, the desire to fulfill our potential leads us to the next higher level. As the illustration on the following page shows, the first stages of need deal with physical and psychological survival; later on, the focus is on spiritual development.

Instinct takes charge of helping us meet the first two levels of deficiency needs; it compels us to find the water, food and protection we need for survival and safety. In this we're no different from every other living organism—we're hardwired to survive. Our common path diverges, however, once we've met the challenges of physical existence and develop an ego. Ego allows us to become conscious of ourselves and its executive function directs our actions

Then, as we master our deficiency needs, we gain access to inner resources that are readily available to energize, nourish and fulfill us. Through self-understanding we come to realize what really matters in life. We discover that intuition, our sixth sense, reliably connects us to what will make life most meaningful in any given moment. With the ego no longer driving us, we seem to be pulled by our spiritual purpose to manifest what's best for us, and others. Ultimately, we may come to realize our oneness with all of life.

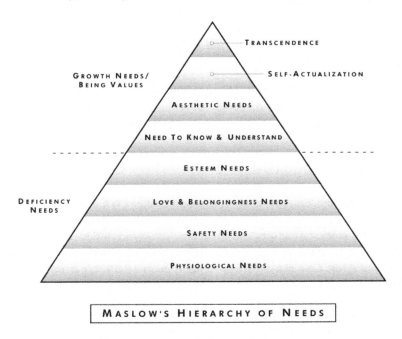

MASLOW'S HIERARCHY OF NEEDS

Not everyone, of course, develops at the same pace and it will appear that some are not developing at all. Maslow's Hierarchy suggests that a large number of people will struggle with survival issues their entire life; fewer will master their deficiency needs and engage higher levels of need. And only some of these will come close to or attain self-actualization and transcendence.

Most people reading this book already have a good handle on meeting deficiency needs and are awakening to their growth needs.

I can say this with some certainty because this book deals with needs in the Growth Need/Being Values section of Maslow's Hierarchy. If you were primarily concerned with meeting deficiency needs, you simply wouldn't be interested in how to be more fulfilled than you are (a sign of cognitive need) and aesthetic needs wouldn't be on your radar at all.

This is not to say you don't have material or emotional concerns. Of course you do! Meeting these needs, however, is no longer the primary motivation of life; you have bigger fish to fry. The discomfort you feel—the longing for something more deeply satisfying—is a divine discontent. Your soul hungers for you to realize who you are in your largest aspect and calls you to fulfill your potential.

Heeding the Call

What does the call of your soul sound like? What exactly is it telling you? And, can you trust what you hear it saying? We've all heard the stories of saints and insane people who believed God had told them to do some really bizarre stuff. Who wants to be that person? Aren't we asking for trouble to even mention getting a call from our soul?

If I hadn't had such clear examples of calling in my own life, I would have been the first one to agree. My experience, however, is that when we're ready to take on the next level of need, a call is exactly what seems to take place. The call may be clear like the "still, small voice" that Elijah heard or perhaps it's just a vague hunch we feel inclined to follow. Regardless, it offers an invitation to greater fulfillment than we may have dreamed possible.

In the case of my calling to ministry, there was no end to well-timed signs and wonders: Scott Peck's *The Road Less Traveled* coming into my hands, the person sitting nearby in a cafe vomiting on my table, three car accidents in as many days making a total wreck of my car, an earthquake in the same instant that I said Yes. Granted, my soul was starving for a sense of purpose and my mind was set on finding meaning in these events. My ego, however, could not have come up with the conclusion to which they all led.

At the time I received the call to ministry I didn't believe in God and I hated church, so much so that I resisted the notion of being a minister for several years. Once I embraced it, however, I not only loved my work, but I was able to integrate all my prior resistance into great ideas for transforming the whole notion of God and church for the benefit of others who had similar issues with organized religion. Something unknown to my conscious mind seemingly led me to actualize potentials of which I was completely unaware.[2]

The call to meet our soul's needs takes whatever form best gets our attention. As I write this, it's 4:00 in the morning; I woke up about an hour ago and couldn't go back to sleep. The phrase "Heed the call" kept repeating itself in my mind until I decided to heed the call, get up and start writing. Why argue, I reason, with such simple instructions? If what I feel called to do won't obviously harm me or others, I figure there's nothing to lose by going along.[3]

The notion of calling is closely aligned with the intuitive sense of entering a current that gently pulls us along to something more fulfilling. If this sometimes feels more like a tug than a flow it's usually because our ego-mind can't believe we would consider

---

[2] I've told the story of how my paralyzing fear of public speaking was transformed in *Where Two Or More Are Gathered: A New Church for the 21st Century*.

[3] I once participated in an est-like workshop characterized by unreasonable requests. One particular evening session was ending close to midnight and we were asked to return by 8 the next morning, but only after having completed a number of assignments. When someone complained that there wasn't enough time to get everything done and still get some rest, the workshop leader said, "You'll have plenty of time to sleep when you're six feet under."

doing something *it* can't control. So, it floods us with doubt and fear. And we're so used to being pushed around by the ego's "shoulds" and "should nots," we don't question it. You can tell if your soul's call doesn't come from your ego by the way you don't feel you're being ordered around. Your soul always grants you the right of refusal. It's persistent, though. Like a telephone on automatic dial, the soul keeps calling and, if you don't pick up, it leaves messages—when you're ready, you'll listen.

The Big Questions Revisited

Who are you? By now I hope it's clear that you are much more than anything you can imagine: You have a body, but you are not exclusively a body. You have thoughts and emotions, but you are not these either. Your whole self includes and transcends your physical and psychological "selves" and is connected beyond any notion of self to the entire universe.

What are you here for? Your mission, should you choose to accept it, is to become what you are in all its fullness. As you partake of the bounty of your whole self, your pleasure spreads to the world.

What should you do with your life? Recognize the needs you have at your current stage of development and intend to meet them. It doesn't matter at which level you find yourself; each one offers you the opportunity and challenge to explore and grow according to your current need. And, when you align your actions with fulfilling this need, you'll experience the congruence with life purpose commonly referred to as happiness. Then, when that need has been fulfilled, you'll be called to the next level, until you *are* the fullness you've been seeking.

What do you want now that you're growing up (now)? You may not consciously know the exact label for this state, but let's just say it's whatever your whole self-soul truly, foolishly, wildly longs to be! Your intuition is already guiding you there (here).

Your Aesthetic Needs

Now I walk in beauty
Beauty is before me
Beauty is behind me
Above and below me.
~ **Native American song**

For those who live, move, and have their being at the level of aesthetic needs, beauty is the prime directive. Beauty—both in idea and expression—is what really matters most to you.

Don't get me wrong; someone whose aesthetic needs aren't primary may enjoy a work of art, but for different reasons. "It looks just like the spot where we always picnic," a friend recently told me about a painting of mine he admired. He decided to buy it (yea!) and gave it to his girlfriend for Christmas. Now, when they look at the painting, my friend tells me, they share memories of good times spent together. For my friend the painting fills his primary need for love and belongingness.

For me, however, it was a completely different story. Making the painting had been a mind-altering experience of dazzling sunlight and dark shade, of color and harmony, rhythm and pattern. After completing the work, I still found the painting visually interesting. Certain areas seemed bothersome, while others fascinated me. The subject of the painting, a path to a Lake Michigan beach, was barely of consequence to me. The meaning of the same painting to me and my friend clearly differed according to our level of need.

Interest, too, is largely a function of need. We pay attention to the things we want or need and find other stuff fairly boring. In the 1970s, long before I became aware of my aesthetic needs, I would occasionally usher for performances of the Atlanta Symphony Orchestra. A guy I was seeing would invite me as a sort of cheap date. A musician, he enjoyed the concerts, but the interminable movements of symphonic music put me to sleep. A music appreciation course (also taken to impress the young man) showed me more of how to listen, but it wasn't until 30 years later that I finally began to understand and want to listen to classical music.

Around the same time that I began painting seriously, I started becoming more attentive to art forms of all kinds. I recognized kinship with other painters as well as composers, photographers, poets, musicians, even certain "body-sculpting" fitness trainers. The fact that we used different media didn't seem to matter; we were all in the same boat—making Art with a capital A. And I could see that none of us was fooling around. This was not playful dabbling but committed work.

Just as an ancient hunter's physical survival depended upon finding food, an artist's spiritual survival depends upon making art. The motivation is different, but the intent is the same—to fill the need that's present at the level of each one's development. The hunter who failed to find and take down his prey might starve to death; the physical life of an artist who doesn't meet her aesthetic needs may go on, but it won't be as meaningful to her as it might be otherwise. To have a life worth living, she must make what she considers beautiful.

Different Strokes

An entire branch of philosophy is devoted to the study of aesthetics. I daresay, however, that if you're approaching or living at the level of aesthetic need, you're likely engaged in your own research on the subject. My own exploration in this vein has led me to appreciate what others have to say about what constitutes beauty—say, for example, the satisfying proportions of The Golden Mean—but I've concluded that the old adage holds true: Beauty is in the eye of the beholder. Each artist has her own way of perceiving beauty and a unique style for expressing it.

As I've mentioned, I come from an artistic family. At one time or another, my four siblings and I have all been devoted to getting our aesthetic needs met; our styles, however, are quite distinctive. For example, we each need our living environments to be visually pleasing.

One sister has a great sense of color and exquisite taste in textiles. A new Romanian rug or piece of Indian fabric will inspire her to repaint the interior of her home, a ritual she repeats at least every couple of years. My younger brother, who was for many years a painter and ceramic artist, installs artifacts he finds in the street or junkyards—stuff I might not look at twice—to create a living space quite different from my sister's. My older brother, who is a writer and visual artist, has built his own home in which you would find counters and shelves all made with distinctive curves that resemble shapes in his early block prints. My other sister, a poet, and I are perhaps less deliberate in our home decorating but if you visited our homes, you'd nonetheless find evidence of our taste and style

My father's aesthetic needs motivated him to make a big fuss about the appearance of our living room at home. He'd spend his hard-earned money to buy good quality prints—Lautrec, van Gogh, Eakins—which he meticulously framed by hand and hung on the walls. He chose the fabric for slipcovers and curtains, as well as the large braided rug.

Frequently, aesthetic trouble in our household would center on shoes and clothing left lying around the living room by careless kids. After school, I'd usually come in and kick off my shoes. When I went out to play, if I remembered, I'd shove the shoes under the couch because there was a rule about stuff in the living room. If I left the room forgetting to hide them, my father would throw each one in a different closet or out the back door. Getting ready for school each morning often required significant time to look for shoes. I thought it was a game but it was one my father took seriously.

People trying to meet their aesthetic needs can seem really difficult to live with to everyone else. I mean, really—your own kids' shoes?! But now I see that my father really *needed* the living room to *look* the way he had designed it. His well-being—or as much of it as he could muster—depended upon a particular visual order. I have my own version of the same need.[4]

People often stand in awe of those with artistic talent, but they're also a bit suspicious of those who possess it. Artistic temperaments are portrayed as eccentric, fussy, difficult or downright psychotic (He cut off his ear?!) And, watch the Jackson Pollock biopic; you'll see van Gogh wasn't alone in the extreme mood swing department.

The so-called artist types in my high school also stood out. Introverted and inaccessible, they withdrew into their own odd clique. Clearly, they weren't obsessed with fitting in the way I was; even at that young age, they had different needs to fill. It was more important to those kids to express their own style than to conform to the conservative fads and fashions of that time.

If an artist is a sort of oddity, an artist's need for beauty may also seem strange, impractical and superfluous. To people who live primarily at the level of deficiency needs, aesthetic concerns appear more like quirky options than real needs.

An artist is a curiosity to others for the very fact you want to spend so much time engaged with something to which most adults is

---

[4] My mother, on the other hand, didn't have an aesthetic bone in her body. She didn't care what the house looked like, but for her own need or reasons—not upsetting my father, not wanting to buy us new stuff—she encouraged us to get the shoes out of my father's sight.

considered child's play. If, to the casual observer, your art-making "looks like fun," it's usually because of some dim memory of a childhood experience; you seem "lucky" to be able to goof off like a kid. "Needs? Schmeeds!" says the 9–5 working onlooker.

No wonder it's challenging to acknowledge you've come to a stage in life when art is what really matters to you. When many of the people closest to you (and most of humankind) aren't going to understand your commitment to meeting your aesthetic needs, it's fairly natural to minimize or even dismiss the urge you have to make art. However, because your needs don't just go away but rather become more urgent, it's important to acknowledge them. My father might have been (a lot) more skillful in getting his aesthetic needs met had he been able to acknowledge that they were his real needs and not just quirky options.

As adults, no one else can fill our needs for us. If where you're at is the level of aesthetic needs, it's up to you to figure out what you need aesthetically and give it to yourself. It's your responsibility and it's okay that doing so will give you pleasure.

Aesthetic Needs & the Artist—You!

While many people appreciate having an appealing place to live or pretty things, aesthetic needs are more than a set of conditions we place on the world that things be attractive or nice in a certain way. Our aesthetic needs go much deeper than the enjoyment of material beauty; they're actually spiritual in nature, connecting us with an invisible realm of art ideas.

Those for whom art-making becomes a vocation may have the experience of being called that's usually associated with religious service. (As suggested in the previous chapter, the "call" originates within, as an indication from our whole self of a need to experience Something More of our own potential.) The calling to "do art" I perceived on three consecutive sleepless nights in 2002 was every bit as clear as my calling to become a minister. While it took me about six months to figure out what it meant to me to "do art," this kind of transformation can happen in the proverbial "twinkling of an eye."

Yasharel Manzy, an Atlanta-based painter, describes on his website how he had been years working in a non-art related business. Then, in 1990 ...

> While strolling through a gallery a painting with a French scene caught my attention. There I was glued to the floor and frozen. A few moments later this incredible feeling overwhelmed me. I found myself in the crossroads of my life, and I knew there was no turning back. At that time I was a partner in business in Atlanta. To be able to change my banal way of life and go where my heart was that afternoon I decided to change my ways and to become a painter. Now it is very clear that I almost had no part in the transformation that was taking place that day. The following day I changed my office from a place of business into a studio. [5]

Manzy continues to work as a prolific, successful artist.

Whether or not you've experienced this kind of calling, I suspect you're already aware of having certain needs by virtue of the fact that you're still reading this book. You seem to be interested in the questions this book asks, and in some cases, answers. So if I'm correct, it's also likely that you are an artist, either in practice or *in potentia*.

You may have believed until now that you qualify as an artist because you have some kind of artistic talent. You can draw,

---

[5] www.YasharelManzy.com.

perhaps, and your drawing looks like the subject. Or, maybe you have a flair for color, and when you put certain colors together, they work. Or, you tell stories well and like to write. People admire what you do with your talent, and from their admiration you conclude that you do have some skill that others don't, and people with the skill you have are called artists.

Or, you may have believed you were not *really* an artist. Maybe there was a time when you did draw or paint but no one particularly admired what you did, so you concluded that you didn't have the necessary talent for art. You slogged through music lessons but never did anything more than play in the high school band. Yet still you find yourself interested in art. Perhaps now you consider yourself a patron, collector, or a supporter of "the arts."

My definition of an artist, however, springs not from talent-related issues. Someone may have the facility to render likenesses, or play a tune, but feel little interest or need to do so. This person is not an artist. But if you are someone with an attraction for art, art is likely attracted to you. And chances are good you actually are an artist, albeit one with an as yet untapped potential. Since to some extent, any artist has as-yet-untapped potential, we're all in the same boat, more or less.

An artist's primary *raison d'être*, or purpose, is the fulfillment of his or her aesthetic needs. One *is* an artist by virtue of the fact he or she perceives the existence of aesthetic needs. An artist finds meaning and, ultimately, satisfaction by pursuing the fulfillment of aesthetic needs. Artists fulfill their aesthetic needs by creating beauty, harmony, order, symmetry and the like. In other words, by making art, artists fulfill their life purpose.

Artists sometimes confuse fulfilling their life purpose by *making* art with making a living *from* their art; i.e. earning income from sales or performance. When this happens, attention and energy may drop from the level of Maslow's Hierarchy where aesthetic needs motivate action down to the lower levels of the basic needs. It's often because of this that many artists feel frustrated. They do not do "their" art, but only what they believe the market will approve of and compensate.[6]

One consequence of this confusion is the profound discontent with life in general that some artists believe is their lot in life. Professional artists often excuse their unhappiness by looking forward to a time when they will do more of what they want to do, say, after they retire. Yet, many retired professionals, as well as those who come to art-making later in life, neglect their artwork. They may think that to be retired means not having to work at all. Having sold their art for so long, they've forgotten the joy of creating for its own sake, or more accurately, for the fulfillment of their further aesthetic development.

This is a mistake! Maturing means becoming all that you're capable of becoming; more than simply being what it's easy to be, but what you *can* be and *should* be. For those of us baby boomers who grew up with Maynard G. Krebs' squeamishness about work, along with a myriad of labor saving devices, work may be something you shouldn't really *want* to do at all. Who among us hasn't had the thought that the sooner we can make enough money and not have to work, the better off we'll be? While our culture broadcasts this message every day, it's one that misses the point of our being alive in the first place.

If an artist does not work and make what Buddhists call "right effort" at the appropriate level of need, life will not seem worthwhile. Sure, you have to eat. But living your life as a frustrated, unfulfilled artist because you believe you must exclusively serve your basic needs instead of your higher ones, is a

---

[6] Why is the creative staff on "Mad Men" angry? Because they're pleasing clients, not making art.

fundamental confusion. It's what people mean when they talk about "making a dying" instead of "making a living." To make a life worth living means acknowledging you have a purpose, and working to fulfill all of your needs, including your highest ones. For an artist it means working to serve your purpose by making art that you deem valuable.

George Bernard Shaw wrote, "I want to be thoroughly used up when I die, for the harder I work the more I live." Work of the sort he describes is the only way to a truly fulfilled adulthood and the only way to actualize our human potential. While I don't suggest you quit your day job tomorrow, it's important to realize that to be a fulfilled artist, you must develop the habit of putting art-making at the top of your daily to-do list, ahead of the day job and before common notions of retirement.

I hope I've sold you on the notion that you are an evolving being: Having become aware of your aesthetic needs, your primary purpose is to somehow fulfill your evolutionary potential. But if you're not sure about that, if you believe your life is simply a roll of the dice, you still have the option of imbuing it with a sense of meaning, value, and purpose. Ultimately, your life means whatever you decide it means, is as valuable as you want to make it, and as purposeful as you will allow it to be.

Your needs are important—at least as important as other peoples'! Why not let meeting them be the primary purpose in your life? And, if you agree, why limit yourself to your basic needs when there are other, more compelling ones? I believe you'll find the more you give yourself what you need most, the more you will have to contribute to others. Bottom line: If you know or even merely suspect you're an artist, you owe it to yourself and the world to make the art you need and want to make!

Soulful Changes

The fates lead them that will.
Them that won't they drag.
~ **Seneca**

Contrary to popular belief, getting needs met is hardly, if ever, a matter of forcing ourselves to do so. Our willingness to change is as natural as taking the next breath—it requires no thought. Yet, because we do *think* about change, we're often confused into believing our ego's thoughts that we can and must be the change agents in our lives. Instead of trusting the evolutionary impulse that's guided human development to this point, our ego-mind, with its own willfulness, over-rides our fundamental natural willingness to evolve.

When nature (or fate) seems to drag us through the mud, it's usually because our mind has refused what might otherwise be a journey of discovery and fulfillment. Yet the sometimes-broad life changes that want to happen are exactly what would make us feel satisfied with our life—if we'd only let them. This book is all about creating the space in which those soulful changes that *want* to happen may do so.

Making soulful changes is not so much a matter of determining "I will get my aesthetic needs met," as welcoming and entertaining the actions that are the meeting of our need. In other words, doing what wants to be done by us. When we're hungry, our basic need to survive impels us into the action of finding food. In a similar way, we're already poised to meet our other needs too. So what if we simply set out each day to attune ourselves to what our life requires at the level of our deepest need?

It's already in our genetic makeup to respond to life in this way. How else would we have developed since the earliest days of the human race? Our hunting and gathering ancestors didn't force themselves to get up in the morning and go to work; finding food and eating came naturally and established the order of their daily lives. (Not so today, of course; finding food is mostly a matter of sniffing around the kitchen to see what's in the cupboard or fridge —that's why we have room in our life for fulfilling other needs.) Since our needs simply represent who we are at our particular stage of life—whether they are basic needs or growth needs—they are also already inspiring us to take appropriate action. It's no accident you've become interested in art-related topics.

If life boils down to the experience of meeting needs as they present themselves, and if we are already primed to get those needs met, why does it seem so hard to do so? Again, our biggest problem lies in our own mind. Our thoughts, emotions, and the unhappy dramatic tales we tell about them often convince us that evolution doesn't occur naturally or easily.

The storyteller is the ego, of course. It or "I" casts itself in the role of generalissimo in all our affairs: Change can't just happen; it must be strategically planned. In order to be successful, "I" must make a long list of specific things that you must do. Can you imagine your far-distant, primitive ancestors getting up each morning with such a to-do list? 1. Find tree; 2. Carve club; 3. Beat the bushes with club; 4. Etc. Of course not! We assume—and it was likely the case—that they simply got up with a hungry belly and did what needed to be done to assure their survival for another day. Why invest energy making a club on a day when a trap would work better?

Our more primitive ancestors were fortunate perhaps; that their brain size didn't quite allow for the sort of mental gyrations that result in the self-conscious human creature we are today.[7] Egos do represent progress in human evolution but they get quite confused

---

[7] But, then again, our forefathers and –mothers didn't get to do much else besides hunt and gather—and occasionally draw on the walls of their cave.

at times. As we develop beyond getting our basic needs met, part of our evolutionary task is to reckon with this confusion. When not following its own agenda, ego serves an important function in need-fulfillment and, as we'll see, soul can offer it gainful employment in service to this higher purpose.

In the Beginning

The changes your soul wants to make to get aesthetic needs met can be a lot of fun. Give a kid a harmonica and he'll have a good time blowing on it. Give her a brush and pots of paints and she'll love putting stripes of red, yellow and blue on the page. Dressing up and imaginative play-acting are the very stuff of childhood. As adults with a newly discovered call to make art, we frequently begin with a child's enthusiasm.

In the first months after I began painting (at age 52), I'd wake up each morning and, before coffee, run to my easel to see what I'd accomplished the day before. Sometimes I'd pick up a brush and start painting having completely forgotten to eat breakfast. I devoted every spare minute to some aspect of my newfound passion. If I wasn't actually pushing paint around I was reading art books, ordering supplies, looking at other artists' work, or simply looking for the next thing to paint.

I'd also leap at the opportunity to paint with a more experienced friend, my first "art buddy." Like a puppy clamoring to play with an older dog, I didn't understand why she seemed to balk at planning our outings. She'd cancel or reschedule, grumble about how much trouble it all was and, when we actually did paint, nothing she did pleased her. My enthusiasm apparently inspired her to remember her own beginning art impulse, but it also irritated her. She likely knew then what it's taken me a few years to realize—that a long-term relationship with art-making isn't necessarily fun or easy, for the ego is, above all else, a first-rate misery maker.

While fulfillment of our needs naturally wants to happen, we must also apply ourselves to the task. In order to produce works of art, we must do the *work* of art. (It's in the doing that our aesthetic needs are fulfilled.) And, just as life can be difficult, making a life of art can be hard. As Scott Peck reminds us, we humans fall prey to entropy and apathy, especially when it comes to fulfilling our soul's needs. We may realize we need to make art and long to make art and still avoid doing the work that art requires of us. Our ego mind convinces us that other things are more important.

In collusion with our individual ego, contemporary culture also seems determined to keep us from doing the challenging work of making a meaningful connection to our soul. Instead it offers us substitute "relationships" instantly made possible by electronic means. Whether it's a fact or a friend we want to be in touch with, if it isn't fun, easy or quick, it isn't desirable.[8] However, whatever "it" is that we think we want from moment to moment often isn't what we really need. This is a tough lesson to learn and I find myself tested every time I open my laptop: I'm easily caught in the World Wide Web, I cannot resist the charms of Facebook, and I'm as addicted as everyone else to email.

When I relocated recently to my winter home in Puerto Rico, I was without access to the Internet for almost a week. I noticed some anxiety; it seemed silly, but I was concerned about losing my online "presence." Would my 235 Facebook friends worry about me or forget me entirely? And, what if someone wanted to buy a

---

[8] Soon no one will remember when researching a fact meant a trip to the library to look in an encyclopedia. Now, every fact you want to know (and much more) is instantly available by consulting Google the Great. In the old days, at least you'd have the trip home from the library to reflect on what you'd learned; today, however, having "gotten" the information you wanted, you're likely to just as easily dismiss it. Instant availability of facts doesn't equate to wisdom.

painting? I might miss some lucrative sale. To compound my misery, I couldn't get a good cell phone signal. I was almost completely disconnected from everything, it seemed.

On the other hand, without the distraction of my BFF's pleasant but totally unrelated postings, I found myself working on my writing project—uninterrupted. A steady stream of good ideas started to flow and it was all I could do the keep up with writing them down. It had been years since I'd been so immersed, so in touch with my own inner life, and I couldn't get enough of it. *This is the good life*, I mused.

Then the package containing a mobile broadband stick arrived. In spite of my good writing spell, I'd been so eager for access to the Internet that I had my husband pay big bucks to send it by Express Mail. When it didn't arrive at the scheduled time, I wondered if this was a sign I didn't really need it, but I was also delighted to catch the postman who retrieved the package for me before a long holiday weekend began.

Once I got the device properly installed, however, I discovered the stick provided a very slow connection that, like the cell phone, worked only sporadically. No matter! Acting much like a little white mouse in an experiment in random reinforcement, every once in while I was able to nab a piece of virtual cheese—someone had "liked" an image I'd posted a few weeks before or I received a new "friend" request. In spite of these nibbles, however, most of my time was spent waiting to connect with the Internet. In the four days after getting the stick, I didn't write one word!

After some inner wrangling, I was finally able to limit my use of the stick. The "I" who craved the Internet clearly had a much different agenda than the one that was satisfied by writing. One believed itself to be dependent on something outside itself, while the other was experiencing fulfillment from artistic creating. One was acting from the level of emotional deficiency needs, while the other was clearly motivated by higher being values. Unaware of such an inner dynamic, we can be fooled by our immature thoughts and emotions into believing we're still children. Until we question the different parts of ourselves, we may find ourselves playing victim to quick-fix behaviors that are clearly not going to help us get our real aesthetic needs met. Inquiring along these lines helped me get unstuck from the broadband stick.

When we do begin to question our motivations, we may be able to see, as I was able to in my circumstance, that we've allowed a regressed part of us to control us. I was acting as if my primary need was for connections with others (love and belongingness) when my actual need was to write. My experience of using the Internet was frustrating whereas immersion in the writing was deeply satisfying. Don't get me wrong—I love people! But at this stage of my development, putting people before creating is to ignore my soul's most pressing need, miss the fruits of fulfilling it, and stunt my growth.

A loving discipline—a kind of internal parental control—keeps us on track. Truly effective discipline is never imposed from the outside; instead, it comes from a deep desire to live fully and grow. In growing we become a disciple of our own unfolding potentials instead of a slave to old needs that we've already mastered. While we may occasionally indulge our "inner child" with the comfort of familiar treats, maturing people love themselves by engaging in disciplined action.

"Love," writes Scott Peck, "is the will to extend ourselves to support or nurture one's own or another's spiritual growth." It's up to us to look inside ourselves to find that love. And once we let love win, the will to extend ourselves out of our ego's comfort zone allows us to establish new soulful practices that allow our whole self to emerge fully.

The Seven Habits of Deeply Fulfilled Artists are examples of practices designed to nourish your soul's aesthetic hunger. I think of them as soul food. To the extent that you feed your soul with these helpful habits, you'll continue to grow and develop along spiritual lines. Eventually, as your aesthetic needs are satisfied, however, you may come to view these practices as no longer necessary. You'll perhaps go on to have other needs and will long for their fulfillment. But for now, these soulful practices will help satisfy your most compelling need—to make art.

Resistance

While part of us acknowledges the need to grow, as I've just described, other parts of us will resist the changes such soul growth brings. The specific whys and wherefores of this are beyond the scope of this book but, generally speaking, resistance is a manifestation of ego manipulation in the form of negative or "impossibility" thinking.

The resistant ego may taunt a growing self with questions like "Who do you think *you* are?" and "Getting too big for your britches, aren't you?" These doses of toxic shame are attempts to put you in "your" place—a familiar identity controlled by ego—instead in the unknown realm of possibility.

The place where the ego feels most comfortable is the regressed state of an identity we've outgrown but which feels so wonderfully familiar we confuse it with home. For example, when offered an opportunity to do something radically different in our lives, we may revert to childhood eating patterns, indulging in what are commonly known as "comfort foods." I wish I had a painting or a paragraph for every big bowl of popcorn I've eaten to assuage a threatened ego! However, if we're sensitive to the demands of our many ego-selves, we may avoid the consequences of acting as if we are less mature or capable than we really are. By making certain efforts, it's possible to sort through the conflicting messages we give ourselves (which we may incorrectly believe come from others) and make choices to act based on what seems to be the highest need of which we are aware.

For those with emerging aesthetic needs, resistance often takes the form of minimizing their importance. The desire to make art, for example, can seem more like an annoyance or indulgence than an opportunity for fulfillment. Women, especially, frequently seem reluctant to pursue art-making, which is often a solitary and serious pursuit. It's particularly hard when those they love are struggling to meet their basic needs. Strongly identified with the role of mother (and to a lesser extent, wife), they're used to setting aside their desires for the wants and needs of others. Even when their children have left the nest, their grandchildren delight and distract them from getting their own needs met. Others, who don't have kids and grandkids, may have spent their adult lives forging other equally sturdy identities they resist setting aside.

One friend of mine, recently turned 60, told me it was scary to her to think of trying to create at this stage of her life. "That's why we have *artists*," she told me one day as she took an admiring stroll around my studio. She went on to explain she doesn't want to take responsibility for her creative ideas. "I like keeping them in my head—that way they don't get screwed up." How many of us are in the same boat? We have good ideas but little confidence in our ability to bring them into manifestation. It seems easier to stay in familiar roles and leave creating to others.

The rumblings of an increasingly hungry soul threaten to disrupt what we've worked hard to establish. Who are we if not who we've previously thought ourselves to be? What happens if we give up the roles that have defined our adult lives? Given the uncertainty involved in making changes, it's easy to cling to familiar obligations and routines. Still, our aesthetic growth needs pull on us like a powerful magnet. Life usually finds a way to overpower our resistance to change. Inertia may be digging in its heels but, in what may seem to be a cosmic tug of war, our soul's overriding purpose pulls us toward fulfillment.

The Greek philosopher Seneca reminds us: When Life wants something more from us than we've been able or willing to give, adversity may appear to evoke it—the unexpected death of a loved one, a traumatic accident, an illness. Often as not, we cry, "Not fair!" and go along only because we have to, with a lot of kicking and screaming, or more quietly, in despair. Yet, while we may hate every aspect of being dragged over the coals, if we are willing to give up believing we are victims, we see that our essential self has not been harmed. Then, our new awareness shines like a pearl of great price and we get on with a new life.

So it is that, sooner or later, everyone has the opportunity to become what he or she was created to be. Circumstances that seem to conspire against you reveal your tremendous inner resources. At the very least, you may leave a legacy of endurance; at the very most, your creativity brings great ideas to expression in the world.

Life's purpose for you is identical with your purpose for Life. The discontent you feel in your daily life is simply your need to grow making itself known—the desire for something more to be fulfilled in and through you. Your desires, in fact, are the key to this deep need; some would say your desires are "God knocking at the door of your heart." However you conceive of an ultimate reality—and even if you don't—the important thing is to acknowledge your desires are key to unlocking the door to your purpose.

Occasionally, a message pops up on my computer screen to tell me that a certain software program has updates available. "Will I allow the change?" it inquires. If I click on the "yes" button, the machine downloads the new information from the Internet. Your desire, longing, and need to create beauty in the world are a request for updates in your experience. When you agree to allow the changes, support for making the soulful changes presents itself. When you resist, the pesky pop-up message will insert itself with unending patience, urging you to reconsider.

The seven soul food practices that follow are intended to nourish your soul's desire to fulfill your aesthetic growth needs. You don't *have to* do any of them, but you'll find yourself increasingly satisfied with your life when you do. Are you willing to allow the soulful changes that Life is inviting you to make? Read on ....

PART TWO

SOUL FOOD

Habit #1

Listen Deeply

Before I can tell my life what I want to do with it,
I must listen to my life telling me who I am.
~ **Parker J. Palmer**

A Deeply Fulfilled Artist makes it a practice to listen deeply to the longings of her innermost self. She honors her need for beauty in all forms. She follows her intuition to deeper understanding of her aesthetic needs.

When a caterpillar spins out silk to create the cocoon in which an amazing metamorphosis will take place, it's unlikely she's considering her behavior with much awareness—she's acting instinctually. Something deep within her, a life force, impels her to make those changes that will fulfill her potential. She doesn't hesitate to wrap herself in the cocoon of her own creation. Then she turns to a gooey mush for a while and eventually, transformed, emerges as a beautiful butterfly. Without a care in the world, she flies off to pollinate some sweet smelling flowers.

As instinct leads the caterpillar and other living creatures to fulfill their basic needs, intuition guides us humans to realize our higher growth needs and being values. Fulfilling our aesthetic needs is not difficult when we connect with our intuition. Intuition speaks quietly, however, and we must listen deeply to hear the voice of our deepest and most essential self.

Deep listening, like a powerful laser, focuses your attention, allowing it to penetrate beyond the layers of ego and reach the well of clear insight, ideas, and inspiration that exists deep within you. When you partake of these fresh ideas, you find yourself able to move more easily and effortlessly in the direction of your own transformation and fulfillment of your soul's most profound needs.

The best way I know to practice the habit of listening deeply is to set aside a regular time for solitude and quiet. Whether you commit yourself to a formal meditation practice or take a walk by yourself once a day—each has its benefits—removing yourself from distractions is paramount. Intuitive insights whisper and they're hard to hear when there's a lot of competing noise. So, for whatever period of time you intend to devote to listening deeply, turn off the Twitter and dumb down the smart phone.

If you have a meditation practice, you're probably already in the habit of withdrawing yourself from the demands of daily life for a period of time each day. If you don't already meditate and would like to learn, this is an excellent way to open to intuitive leanings. While there are many different meditation techniques you could try, the most straightforward of these instructs you to simply follow the ins and outs of your breathing for a specified time—five minutes if that's all you can manage. With practice, meditation has the effect of calming your mind. Among other beneficial effects, such as lowering blood pressure, your thoughts become less intrusive and the content of your unconscious mind may become more available to you. There's a cumulative effect, too; meditators may find they become more focused and intelligent the longer they meditate.[9]

If you're not inclined to take up meditation, there are other effective ways to practice the habit of listening deeply. One way that works well for me I discovered in Julia Cameron's *The Artist's Way* (a must-read for anyone seeking to meet their aesthetic needs). Cameron suggests a daily practice of "morning pages": three handwritten sheets of uncensored stream of consciousness writing. In writing morning pages, you actually learn to listen to the content of what's present in your mind. I usually do this writing while I'm still in bed, before I've had any coffee or breakfast. I write about whatever comes up. To begin

---

[9] My IQ increased by more than 20 points after I'd been meditating for about 10 years!

with there's often a lot of disjointed thoughts and complaints generated by my conscious mind. Then, dream fragments and other vague recollections and, sometimes, when I've gotten the other stuff out of mind, a gem of pure inspiration may appear on the page. Always, I have three pages of *something* and I can congratulate myself for having accomplished *that.*

Sometimes, if I'm not being disciplined enough to meditate or write morning pages, I simply indulge in a bit of "muse" time. While it may be viewed by others as goofing off or daydreaming, muse time is the opportunity I take to sit around and do nothing but muse about things: Life, the day, what I want, what I'm unhappy about, and so forth. Often, while musing, I'll become aware of good ideas. Like wisps of cloud floating in the breeze, to catch hold of them you have to be gazing mindlessly at the sky. Muse time is hard to come by in today's world. It's so easy to fiddle with some electronic media device instead; however, time spent checking emails and Facebook doesn't count as muse time.

Once I started painting, I discovered I could also find the solitude and quiet for listening deeply while doing my art. And the more interior silence I accessed, the better I painted. Of course, this requires limiting the distractions in your art-making environment. If you share a studio with others or like chatting on the phone or listening to the radio while you make your art, you'll want to set aside another time for your deep listening.

Deep listening sounds simple—and it is—however, as with many worthy endeavors, it's not necessarily easy to accomplish. As much as you might like to hear what your intuition has to tell you, your ego may prefer that you not. Be prepared: As soon as you decide to install quiet time in your routine, you'll find a million other things that demand to be done at exactly the same time. Suddenly you'll find it imperative that you check your email every five minutes and answer your cell phone every time it chimes.

With practice, however, you'll come to see how distractions are roadblocks thrown up by your ego to block fulfillment.

Why would the ego do that? Remember the caterpillar? Before turning into a butterfly, she first dissolves her body into mush. If it weren't for the cocoon, the gooey mess formerly known as caterpillar might ooze all over the place. No self-respecting ego-based identity consents to its annihilation; further, it's reluctant to admit there's anything to "us" besides the sense of "I" that is the ego. Perhaps it's no wonder that the ego tries to distract us from our own fulfilling transformation.

In spite of the ego's beliefs to the contrary, we too have cocoons. Our whole self forms a larger context in which our souls have the space to unfold to their greatest potential, far beyond what the ego requires for its sense of security. And that's a good thing!

With practice and an increasing ability to hear the voice of your intuition, you'll start to cherish your deep listening time. The power of those distracting ego-intrusions diminishes as your attention is drawn inward. As you learn to trust and abide in the guidance provided by your intuition, your approach to life subtly becomes less fragmented.

For example, I make it a habit to ask for inner direction whenever I go painting outdoors. I live part-time on a small island that has many attractive beaches where I can work and tourists who are inclined to buy paintings of them. While my ego attunes itself to the sales potential of a painting venue, this rarely satisfies deeper aesthetic needs. The whole time I'm looking for a painting spot, I'm trying to figure out which spot would "sell" best, and when I find one, part of me is second-guessing my choice. When I get down to painting, if it's with an eye to sales, my judgment of what constitutes a pretty picture often produces a contrived piece. Trying to suss out all the angles is exhausting.

My preferred practice, then, is to *not* decide ahead of time on a strategic destination. Instead, when I head out in my car I simply observe where it seems to want to turn, left or right. Then I go that way until it wants to turn again, and so on until I arrive at some place or other. Then I set up my easel and start to work. I select my subject by seeing where my attention is drawn and apply paint in a similar manner. I know it sounds odd, but this deep listening approach has proven to be a very effective way to work. The paintings done in this manner have a loose, energetic quality and I love making them.[10]

You may wonder how things get done if your ego isn't acting as change agent, but marvelous occurrences take place without your having to make extraordinary efforts. What we call "luck" or "good fortune" is actually our experience of the way things work at the level of our unified existence. When you listen deeply to your whole self, you become attuned to your soul's needs; your process of living takes you effortlessly to the inner and outer places where those needs will be met. You'll discover that the experience of your whole self is, in and of itself, tremendously satisfying. Applied to specific needs, it seems miraculous how the right resources—people, places, ideas, and money—apparently manifest themselves when we listen deeply within ourselves.

Listening deeply to both your need for beauty and your desire to make art, you may realize some potent changes begin to take place. You're not exactly who you once thought you were. And, since even the most imaginative caterpillar cannot fully comprehend where her butterfly self may travel, you may feel somewhat timid about committing yourself to meeting your

---

[10] Many years ago I tested my intuitive guidance system when traveling from my home near Kansas City to visit a friend in Springfield, MO, a city I'd been to only once before, with only her street address for reference. Following my intuition, I made my way off the interstate highway and made various turns until I found myself in a neighborhood that "felt" right. After a few minutes, though, I hadn't yet found my friend's street. Realizing I was about to be late, I stopped to ask directions at a 7-Eleven®. I was only two blocks away!

aesthetic needs. Yet, once your soul has said Yes, even when your heels drag a bit, you'll find the rest of you is already on the way.

***

Habit # 1 of a Deeply Fulfilled Artist invites you to Listen Deeply. This implies that you:

- Set aside time and space for the solitary enjoyment of your whole self on a regular basis.

- Listen deeply for an increasing attraction to beauty and desire to make art that may indicate your aesthetic needs want fulfilling.

- Observe what activities seem to keep you from establishing a deep listening practice. See if you can identify the level of need to which these belong.

- Exercise your intuition to access deeper levels of self-understanding.

Reflections

Intuition is sometimes referred to as a sixth sense, helpful when the other five are preoccupied with getting basic needs met. I think of my intuition as connecting me to a largely unconscious higher self, which is in turn a part of a universal creative impulse. Intuition doesn't always reveal a concrete answer, but one usually comes away from an intuitive exercise with a deeper sense of one's self and what really matters.

Here's a simple way to prime your intuition. In your quiet time, ask yourself the following questions, one at a time, and quickly write down your response. Then ask yourself the same questions again, and again. Watch what your intuition brings to your attention. Sometimes you'll receive helpful insight about yourself. Other times you might receive a specific idea of something you want to do or get. Over time, you'll come to trust the call of the quiet voice of your intuition to do or be Something More.

What are you grateful for?

What do you desire?

What do you aspire to?

What do you dream of?

What do you hope for?

What would you love to happen in your life?

Name 100 things you'd love to happen in your life before you die.

Name 100 things you'd love to create artistically before you die.

Name 10 things you'd love to have happen this year.

Habit # 2

Give Yourself What You Most Need

You can't always get what you want; but if you try
sometimes, you just might find you get what you need.
~ **Rolling Stones**

A Deeply Fulfilled Artist sets aside culture's notions of success in favor of her own need-based definition. She recognizes her purpose lies in meeting her needs and makes fulfilling artistic needs a daily priority. When called to make art, she says, "Yes."

On I-85, the interstate highway in Gwinnett County, Georgia where I lived until a couple of years ago, there are two large water tanks. Some county official in this, one of the once fastest growing counties in the United States, had the bright idea to paint each water tank with encouraging slogans. "Gwinnett is Great" and "Success Lives Here" appears on the opposite side of each tank as if to make sure the message really hits home. While sitting in the often-gridlocked traffic of this indisputably great county's 16-lane expressway, I spent many hours pondering, in particular, the meaning of "Success Lives Here."

What is the success to which the slogan refers? I wondered. I imagine it means financial success. At one time, before the tide of legal and illegal immigrants rolled in, Gwinnett had the largest per capita income of any county in the nation. Success meant enough money to build huge subdivisions filled with huge homes and huge malls that would supply their furnishings. Now, with the economics of the area a bit less certain, and those trophy homes with For Sale signs on their less-than-manicured lawns, one wonders if anyone at the county offices is reconsidering those water tanks and a more lasting definition of success.

Because of my family history, I often defined success in terms of my father's happiness. I was successful if I managed to pour him a beer with the right amount of foam on top; if the boy I was dating enjoyed listening to my father's jazz records; if, if, if…. It took me a long time to define success in terms of my own happiness and to give myself the gift of having success live "here" in my life.

On the other hand, my dad seemed to equate success with having enough money to buy beer, cigarettes, and Toulouse Lautrec prints for the living room wall. For his life to be bearable, these things were necessities. After all, he'd always stepped up to assume responsibility for his family. He'd forgone much he thought frivolous, always with an eye to economy. (When my father went to purchase the only brand new car he'd own, a sturdy Dodge Dart, he got a lower price by having the air conditioning unit removed. In Georgia, where the summers sizzle, he had them take out the A/C!) He did seem to feel that certain pleasures were his due and he managed to buy what he wanted with the weekly allowance my mother doled out to him from his Lockheed paycheck. In fact, he furnished our entire house with his allowance, which never totaled more than $20.

My point is that we all have different notions of success, and it's up to each one of us to figure out where these notions come from and whether or not they fit who we really are. In my case, I tried for a long time to make my father happy. However, eventually I realized I could not ever succeed in saving my father from himself. In regard to that measure, I was a complete and utter failure!

Having reached this stunning conclusion, I came to embrace an entirely different idea of success: Success is the fulfillment of whatever I really need. If I don't really need something (I'm speaking now in terms of Maslow's Hierarchy of Needs), then having it or not having it is meaningless. "Success Lives Here" when I'm actively engaged in fulfilling needs that are meaningful to my development; that is, when I am living my purpose. Failure occurs only when I neglect my needs, either the basic ones or higher ones as I become aware of them.

What happens when you define success in terms of fulfilling your needs? Almost immediately you'll begin shift your focus from what other people deem to be success to a sense of what really matters to you. This may seem like a small thing but I assure you it is not!

For instance, suppose you are accustomed to judging the success of a painting or poem by the approval rating of whoever your audience happens to be. Your supersensitive radar tells you whether they like it or not before they open their mouths, doesn't it? If you're at all like me when I let others judge my work, and there's anything less than total approval, you're prone to throw in the towel, or at least suffer a fit of pique. Critiques and juried competitions can be pure hell for artists who let others define success for them (unless they happen to win, in which case they risk having sold their artistic soul to the devil!).

But imagine bringing your work forward in another manner altogether, recognizing that simply by creating it, you are fulfilling and fulfilled by your need to make art.

I invite you to make an agreement with yourself to love unconditionally every piece of work you produce. Love it, not because it is "good" or because it "captured the subject" or for any reason other than the fact that it is evidence of your fulfilled need. Acknowledge that you are serving your purpose, the fulfillment of your aesthetic needs. Recognize that every time you write a chapter, make a painting or sing a song, you are actually doing the thing you were put here to do—probably not all of it, but some portion of it. So, you have succeeded in fulfilling your primary goal, your need to make art! You've done it, not to be a success on someone else's terms, not to make money, but for the fulfillment of your aesthetic needs. This, perhaps, is the true meaning of "Art for Art's sake."

Success lives here, in you, right now, as the fulfillment of what you need most. Your job is to continue to discover what you need next and meet that need too. No one else can tell you when you've completed your fulfillment project. But you will know it, feel it in your bones, and give it back to the world in the form of more beauty and a greater good than it has known before.

***

Habit #2 of a Deeply Fulfilled Artist is to Give Yourself What You Need Most. This implies that you:

- Envision your life as a project in which you are committed to fulfilling the needs of your evolving self.

- Cultivate new notions of success based on getting your needs met. Your primary goal is to fulfill your needs.

- When faced with decisions about how to use your time, attention, talent and other resources, get in the habit of checking to see the ways in which your choices align you with or distract you from your purpose.

- Apply the principle of "Secure your own oxygen mask before helping others."

Reflections

How do you imagine your life will be when you are fulfilling your artistic purpose?

The needs of those we love—children, aging parents, spouses—may seem more compelling than our own. Is this true or not true in your experience of getting your artistic needs met?

Especially if we are accustomed to taking care of others' needs, we may unconsciously believe someone else will take care of ours. How would you act differently if you knew no one else besides you could meet your most important needs?

Habit # 3

Do Your Art

Just Do It!
~Nike

> A Deeply Fulfilled Artist makes it her practice to do her art. She gives herself complete permission to do the art she needs to do for the satisfaction of her aesthetic needs. She then "gets to" work.

The Third Habit of Deeply Fulfilled Artists is the perhaps the most obvious of the seven habits described in this book. If you adopt only one of these seven habits as your own, let it be this one. It's the one in which you give yourself permission to do the one thing in the world that will satisfy your most important need. Yes, you "get to" do the thing you must—your art.

When I first began observing the habits of the various artists I know, I was amazed by the amount of not-doing of art that goes on. Artists often speak of doing art as if it is torture rather than something they love. I see how I also avoid doing the thing I love to do best when I groan with guilt, "I've really got to paint today," knowing full well that I probably won't. That "got to" assures that I'll feel bad no matter what I do or don't do.

Resistance is inevitable (as well as futile). Our resistance kicks in precisely because some part of us recognizes that we *must* do art in order to satisfy our deepest needs. So rather than beating ourselves up, let's try to understand what triggers our resistance to what is good for us and explore what to do about it.

Most of us are brought up with notions that we *should* do certain things in order to be good people. Some people respond well to having standards imposed upon them by authoritative people or institutions; many creative people, however, do not appreciate being told what to do. They have their own ideas they long to express; submission to the will of others often seems to them a fate worse than death.

Since they reject some cultural norms, artists sometime appear rebellious. In their eccentricity, they may seem like adolescents who balk at doing anything an adult asks of him, declaring, "You're not the boss of me!" I believe it's a good thing when artists question established authority; creation, after all, derives from the impulse to author *new* works.

Yet, as artists, we may foolishly (and usually unconsciously) thumb our nose at our own inner authority. When we suffer from "blocks," it's often resistance to our own creative impulse that is the problem. To the extent we resist committing to our need to do art, it will seem unattractive, abhorrent, or impossible and we end up avoiding the very thing we want and need.

How then can we reinvent our own strategies so that we move from avoiding the thing we need the most to being a reliably "Just Do It" person? We'll explore several ways in the course of this handbook, but one way to begin short-circuiting this internal saboteur is to cultivate the habit of re-framing the imperative to make art from a punishing "got to" to an inviting "get to."[11]

Once I begin to speak of art-making as an opportunity, not a chore, I begin to look forward to it rather than dreading it. When I give myself permission to do my art, I'm like a deliciously wicked child with my hand in the cookie jar. Other tasks await me, but, first, I'm allowed to—indeed, I must—taste the sweetness of my art. I don't have to paint. I want to! I get to! I plan for it, look forward to it, I Just Do It!

---

[11] I'm indebted to Jill Badonsky, author of *The Nine Modern Day Muses (and a Bodyguard)*, for instilling in me the powerful "get to" re-frame. Replace the burden of "should" with "get to" and watch how much more enjoyable doing art can be.

Habit# 3 invites you to view art-making as a fulfilling opportunity that you "get to" do. That means that with full permission, you:

"Get to" do your art on a regular basis.

What does "art on a regular basis" mean? For Duane Keiser, a representational oil painter, it meant producing a "postcard" painting every day. Keiser's career zoomed along as he posted these realistic gems to his blog and put them up for auction on e-Bay. In 2006 USA Today did a front-page article about him and his name is synonymous with the practice of daily painting, at least in my studio.

From the number of "daily painting" websites that have popped up in the years since that USA Today article, it looks like I wasn't the only artist who reacted by adopting Keiser's practice as their own. It looked to me like a no-brainer: Whip off a little jewel in an hour or less, get it up on the Internet, wait for the $$$ to roll in. Plus, there would be the satisfaction of doing my art on a regular basis. It would be a simple way to paint, market, and enjoy the rewards, wouldn't it?

I know some artists were more successful than I was, but my experiment lasted only a few days. Duane's idea of art on a regular basis simply didn't work for me. My profit-serving motivation, I'm sure, didn't serve my aesthetic need to do art for its own sake. And, since I felt like a failure when I didn't produce the daily painting, I found myself digging up old paintings and posting them to my blog instead of new work. Finally, eBay started charging me to put the work up for auction. The expense of it finally got the best of my willful vanity.

Upon reflection, I learned that while I intend to make art on a regular basis, for me, "regular" doesn't mean every day. It means at least an hour, more like 4–6 times a week. If I create a rigid painting schedule, I know that I will react to it by not painting. (The ego likes nothing more than a good fight!) If, on the other hand, I create a flexible schedule, it's more like an invitation for my muse (who I call the Queen of Happiness & Beauty) to appear, than a demand that "I" paint. When the Q of H&B turns up, I actually paint more than the schedule invites; in practice, hardly a day goes by when her paintbrush isn't working in my hand.

What does doing art on a regular basis mean to you? Play with this question, try on different scenarios, and see what works. Once you discover what "on a regular basis" means to you, you'll do it or you won't—either way, you'll discover something important about your relationship with your art.

"Get to" do your art in a committed fashion.

For one reason or another, I spent many years of my early adult life selling myself short on the commitment front. If you believe that what you do or don't do doesn't matter, commitment is always an issue. Commitment implies you take yourself and your efforts sincerely, allowing for the possibility, at least, that you and they can make a difference in the world.

Making art may sometimes be fun, but it is not a frivolous activity. Your commitment to making art is a commitment to life and to the world. So in my view, if you're going to do your art, it's an opportunity to do it as if the outcome matters to yourself and to others.

The way I see it, everything we do makes a difference; all of our actions and inactions impact the world for better or worse. If I approach my art unconsciously or irresponsibly, that action will impact the world and me in an unconscious and irresponsible way. If I neglect to do my art at all, I am withholding from others and myself something we potentially need or could use in a positive way. The difference we make may not be earth shaking, but it is a contribution, nonetheless, which in turn gives meaning to the way in which we approach doing our art.

Here's what doing art in a committed fashion looks like to me:

- I create a place to work so I can work.
- I create times to work on a regular basis.
- I obtain the materials I need to work.
- I prepare myself physically, mentally, and spiritually to be able to work.
- I aim to produce the most beautiful work of which I'm capable.
- I use the momentum of regular painting, painting in series, and other good work habits to strengthen my commitment.
- I accept support for my efforts from others; I seek instruction when I need it.
- I value my work by completing, signing, showing, and selling it.

"Get to" do your art with a reverently irreverent attitude.

With my history as a somewhat irreverent reverend, I am perhaps uniquely qualified to recommend this approach to making art. Let me be clear that I'm not suggesting you drag religion into your art-making! But I do recommend you hold your practice of making art in high regard, for art is essentially a spiritual undertaking.

Since to me art is a spiritual activity, I find it galling when artists approach it as if there is a religious "right" way to do it. (I once studied with a painting instructor who claimed that pthalo blue is evil, because, like Satan, it makes a mess of everything it touches.)

Spirituality, I have suggested elsewhere[12], is not about right and wrong, but about consciousness.

As I understand it, spirituality is the consciousness of being present in the Now Moment. Call it "flow," or "being in the zone," every time you work with your wholehearted attention, you come into a state in which art arises spontaneously. When I am fully present, it is not so much that "I" paint, in the sense that I am willing every stroke of the brush, as it is that my ego serves Something More, which now expresses itself through me. When I don't condition my art-making with rules, the process absorbs me and painting feels effortless.

As a largely self-taught artist, I've been able to watch my painting ability develop rather quickly without the guidance of a more experienced teacher. In fact, trained artists who admire my style sometimes seek me out for instruction. What's really needed is frequently not more technical advice but a spiritual teaching that encourages practice along the lines of "be here now."

"Get to" have an art life filled with GRACE

I came across a lovely acronym for GRACE in George Leonard's book, *The Life We Are Given.* Leonard offers this as a tool for preparing to do a daily exercise routine, but it can also be applied to your life, as a way of allowing a sense of Something More to enter into your daily artistic existence. I use it to remind myself of what I can do to lead a grace-filled art life. I find it especially helpful when overwhelmed by chaos, confusion, and distraction.

G—Ground: Am I feeling a sense of connection with my body, with my physical surroundings? Am I feeling connected to the Ground of my Being, the invisible realm of Infinite Possibility and

---

[12] See my book, *Where Two or More Are Gathered: A New Church for the 21st Century.*

Meaning? I deepen my sense of grounding through feeling the connection of my feet with the earth beneath me.

R—Relax: Is there tension in my body, in my mind? Where do I feel it? What happens if I choose to let it all go? I relax by focusing attention on my breath. Breathing in, I allow myself to become present to the moment; breathing out, I release and let go all thoughts beyond the breath.

A—Aware: Where is my attention? Is it dwelling in the past or the future—or in my concern for or judgment of another or myself? I become aware of where my attention departs from here and now and simply bring it back to the present.

C—Center: Are my body, mind, and spirit in balance? I touch the center of my body, close my eyes, and invite these three aspects to align with my artistic purpose.

E—Energize: What is my energy level? Am I feeling depressed, overworked? I imagine myself tapping a reservoir of spiritual energy flowing in from the top of my head and earthy energy pulsing up through the soles of my feet. I notice my heart quickening as it circulates oxygen-rich blood to my entire body. I am ready to engage life and all it offers me today.

"Get to" do your art for the rest of your working life.

When my husband and I got married, we were both rather daunted by the notion of a "forever" commitment. But since we were married in a civil ceremony, without the option of writing our own vows, we found ourselves saying "I do" to the "'til death us do part" of a traditional marriage. For a number of years, we'd joke that we'd only agreed to be married for "an indefinite period of time."

Years later, it's a different story. It's clear to both of us that only a forever commitment makes a successful marriage possible: No one is going anywhere—we're here for the long haul. When bailing out is not an option, there's every incentive to find workable solutions to difficulties. There don't have to be, indeed, cannot be, instant remedies. We must find ways to become people who meet the challenges of marriage on a daily basis. As anyone who has been married knows, lots of forgiving of trespasses occurs.

Artists will be greatly served by the intention to approach the doing of art as a lifelong endeavor. If we do this, we won't have to torture ourselves with our perceived failures and shortcomings. We won't have to drive ourselves nuts when someone else appears to have the kind of success that seems to elude us. Not if we're in it for the long haul. What we really want may only be revealed over the full extent of our lifetime.

We will suffer as artists, as human beings, when we attach ourselves to particular outcomes. If our aim, however, is a life well lived, meaning "to the best of our ability," we'll be able to make art in the face of our inevitable limitations. Eric Maisel writes, "To be human is to be constrained." It's our job to overcome those constraints, as we are able, not to beat up on ourselves for our failure to do so. We need to forgive in advance the reality that we will never fulfill all of our potential.

I'm always amazed by reports of how certain people overcome physical challenges to do their art. If I could no longer hold a brush in my hand, I wonder, would I be one of those "foot and mouth" painters? Would I find another way to do art? Or would I simply give up? These are questions that can only be answered in the living of my life. All I know is that I begin in the space of intending to do my art as long as I can; doing the best that I can on a daily basis.

**

Habit # 3 invites you to Do Your Art. This implies that you get to work making art.

- The "10,000 Hour Rule" may or may not apply to mastery of your art. If, however, you dedicate yourself right now to doing whatever it takes to making the art that is yours to make in this lifetime, you will master life and make great headway with your art. How will you know if you've accomplished this? To paraphrase Richard Bach's Reluctant Messiah, "If you're still here, you haven't." Don't practice your art for mastery; practice it because it's what you've chosen to do with your life to meet your aesthetic needs!

- As a kid, I equated work with the chores I had to do in order to collect my allowance each week. I wonder how many of us have been conditioned to do only what was required of us to get paid? If you've worked your whole life at a job you didn't particularly like, of course you look forward to retirement. Art-making, however, is a whole other sort of work with no minimum wage and certainly no retirement age.

- Play with the idea that when you get to a certain age it's okay to *not* be retired. No one encourages you to stop eating food when you're hungry once you've turned 65. Why would you not keep meeting your other needs, especially when they call to you more clearly now that you're more mature? Unless you believe you have to work for someone else, you're the actual boss of your artwork. Consider, however, that you are really employed by the Universe, or Evolution, or whatever concept relates you to the Something More of your human/divine potential. Your work efforts not only fulfill you, but also contribute to the evolution of humankind. Tell Maynard G. Krebs to go jump in a lake.

- Decide that you will work at your art until you are physically or mentally incapable. You don't "got to" work, you "get to" work. So get to work.

Reflections

"Yes, buts..." are what some artists say when asked if they'd like to make more art. For example:

"Yes, I'd love to practice my guitar, **but** what about my day job? —I don't have the time to play."

"Yes, I wish I could paint, **but** there's no room in my house for a studio."

"Yes, writing poems is important, **but** my grandchildren are coming for the summer."

What's your fallback **"Yes, but..."** statement? Is what you're telling yourself and others absolutely true? Who would you be if you got off your "but?" What art could you make today? Will you? Why not?

Where do you hold back from committing to your art?

What would it mean to you to do your art in a committed fashion?

Habit #4

Set Intentions for Your Art Life

Happiness comes of doing things deliberately.
~ **Carlos Casteneda**

A Deeply Fulfilled Artist allows herself to envision possibilities for meeting her aesthetic needs. She aims her intention toward profound creation. She becomes the willing co-creator of virtuous circles that benefit her and others.

The Fourth Habit of Deeply Fulfilled Artists calls upon your capacity for loving yourself so as to change your life for the better.

Many people who desire self-improvement believe changing bad habits into good ones is a matter of willing ourselves to do better than we have done before. We survey our weaknesses and decide to be stronger. If we eat too much, we vow to eat less. If we smoke, we decide to quit.

New Year's and other resolutions often fail to produce desired results, however, because willpower alone cannot obtain the change we seek. In fact willfully browbeating ourselves to improve often backfires and we find ourselves doing more of the stuff we insisted we would never do again.

Why is this so? Simply willing ourselves to do things differently often draws more attention to the very thing we want to be rid of and we desire it even more. At the same time we're negating the life energy we've invested, perhaps unwisely, in certain behaviors or relationships. But, sometimes it's our own willfulness that's been the underlying problem all along. When we resist our own resistance to life by trying to eliminate what we deem undesirable, we unconsciously create a vicious circle of avoidance.

A vicious circle is "a chain of events in which the solution of one difficulty creates a new problem involving increased difficulty." The more someone addicted to chocolate thinks about not eating it, the more important (and desirable) the chocolate becomes. If you're like me, more than one batch of chocolate chip cookies has been baked and eaten after resolving not to. If my motivation for not eating chocolate was to avoid bad side effects from doing so, suddenly, my attempt to enforce abstinence has resulted in a worse situation than before I tried to quit. Not only that, I feel bad about the weakness of my will and the futility of anything ever changing.

What's a better alternative to a vicious circle of avoidance? A virtuous circle of fulfillment. We don't hear a lot about "virtuous circles" but let's define one as "... a chain of events in which the solution of one difficulty creates fulfillment as each subsequent challenge is met with greater ease." We initiate a virtuous circle when, aware that will alone is not enough to bring about lasting change, we bring love of the desired new state into the picture.

Recalling Scott Peck's definition of love, we realize we cannot force love, but we can become willing to extend ourselves to nurture our spiritual (artistic) growth. When we substitute willingness for willfulness, we're simply allowing the changes that growing requires and not making ourselves different simply because we believe we should be improved. There's no forcing current operating here—if presented with a plate of Toll House cookies, there's emotional and mental space to consider the various aspects of the choice to partake or not. Our decision will provide exactly the feedback we need regarding how well we are meeting our needs.

Intentions are most powerful when they originate in the place of our deepest need. Then, they reflect possibilities already inherent in us; for what we truly need is what wants to happen in our lives. Our deepest needs, then, are often just waiting for us to consent to their fulfillment.

There's nothing wrong with "intending" what we think we *want* to happen, however, as long as we don't get too attached to particular results. It's been my experience that we do always eventually get what we *need* for our spiritual development. If we don't really need something, however, even though we may seem to possess it for a while, it will tend go away. Our disappointment over such a loss tends to feed our cynicism and cause unnecessary consternation.

Whenever possible, I find it's less confusing to try to sort out the whole need/want issue *before* forming intentions. Once again, intuition serves as a reliable guide to forming intentions by helping us get past our ego's insatiable appetite—the compensatory desires of our intellect or reactivity of our emotions. When, instead, our intentions express our soul's longing to evolve, we'll see that they create the conditions for a virtuous circle and become even more powerful as we communicate them to others.

A few years ago I stated publicly, "My intention is to create beautiful paintings that will bring joy to the world." Every time I bring this to mind, even when I don't particularly feel like painting, I find myself energized to do what I can in service to this possibility. When I pick up a brush and paint, I fulfill the need I have to make art. The effort comes from my whole heart and mind, not from some "should" I've inherited from my ancient conditioning to please others. I love what I'm doing and so, generally, does the world.

Here are some other positive statements that relate to my intention to create beautiful paintings. Notice how easily my "get to" opportunities transform themselves into intentions:

- I intend to do my art on a regular basis.
- I intend to do my art in a committed fashion.
- I intend to be irreverently reverent about my art.

- I intend to do my art for the rest of my (working) life.
- I intend to have a grace-filled life.

Habit #4 suggests that you Set Intentions for Your Art Life. This implies that you:

- Use not only your head but also your heart in creating changes in your life.

- Focus more on what you want in your life and less on what you don't want.

- State what you want in the form of written or verbal intentions, which you communicate to yourself and to others.

Reflections

What are some vicious circles operating in your life today?

What are some undesired state(s) you've tried to will yourself to avoid?

What desired state(s) or possibilities could you instead intend as a way to transform avoidance into fulfillment?

Create a positive intention to address your largest desire regarding your artistic life.

Habit #5

Use Smart Work Strategies

"Argue for your limitations and, sure enough, they're yours."
~ **Richard Bach**

A Deeply Fulfilled Artist determines how to use her time and energy to best advantage. She builds momentum by capitalizing on her completed accomplishments. She enrolls others to support her efforts by making commitments to them to produce work.

The Fifth Habit of Deeply Fulfilled Artists asks you to work smart. A lot of artists are expert at self-sabotage: We doubt our abilities, criticize ourselves mercilessly, and otherwise disparage our efforts. Perhaps the smartest thing we must learn to do is to root more for our possibilities than argue for our limitations. How do we do this? By using smart work strategies that will support our intentions to make art.

Here's where goal setting comes in. Unlike a more general intention, a goal is something specific you choose to aim for, accomplish or achieve. If you're a classical singer, and it's your intention to make beautiful music with your voice, you might find that one of your goals is "to work with a large opera company." Listen carefully to your intuition and get even more specific by describing which opera company you're drawn to—it's possible this is the one that wants you to be a part of it.

Major or minor, goals help you align your efforts with your intentions and make it simpler to do what needs to be done and not something else. Painter Maud Morgan (1903–1999) writes about an experience of goal setting early in her career:

A book called *Think and Grow Rich* fell into my hands. I read it through several times and followed its instructions: "Decide what you want to do; the time you will allow for doing it; how you will do it; and how much money you want to make. Review this list at least three times a day." This I did. My list was: I want a gallery show. I will concentrate on this for a year. I will sell to the Metropolitan Museum at some point in the near future. And I want to make $2000. Here I frightened myself. I had never sold a painting for more than $25 and was ashamed to have put down this large amount.... But, it all came true.[13]

If you're like me at different times in my life, with goals looming as weighty items on your to-do list, perhaps you've avoided setting specific goals. Since the movie by that name was released a few years ago, creating a "bucket list" has become a popular form of major goal setting. The idea is to outline the major experiences that will give meaningful definition to your remaining days on earth, before you "kick the bucket." For sure, you end up with a set of goals but they bring with them a sense of doom and gloom.

For others, goals signify a destination to be arrived at come hell or high water. You get to your goal but only after many serious offensives or much dodging of bullets on the battlefield of life. If you're like me, you may have given up on setting goals—they're too heavy a burden to carry through your days. After all, isn't life hard enough?

Without goals, however, you wander from day to day without a sense of direction or achievement. Like a horse in pasture, your basic needs may be fulfilled but there's little awareness or growth. You passively await change, which may or may not occur. You eat, sleep, and go through the other motions of life, but it doesn't

---

[13] *Maud's Journey: A Life from Art,* Maud Morgan; 1995, New Earth Publications, Berkeley, CA.

really feel like living. With a goal, however, you saddle up that horse and ride to someplace you've realized you need to go.

Sometimes the reason we avoid making goals for our life is that we fear disappointment. What if we don't get where we said we want to go? What if we get there and it's not what we thought it would be? What if it's the wrong goal? You may believe that if you don't set goals, you won't be sad or mad since those "what ifs" will never come to pass. Guess what? If you don't set goals, you'll just be sad or mad about something else! And you won't have learned what you might have by pursuing your dreams.

After years of my own struggle to make peace with setting goals, I've come to think of them as having a lighter quality than I'd previously experienced. What if goals are nothing more than "sweet obligations" leading to the fulfillment of your need-intention? I first heard this term used by Richard Moss. If I understood correctly, a sweet obligation is work done and efforts made in service of that to which you have consecrated your life. In others words, the fulfillment of your spiritual need.

As my mother aged, I intended that she be cared for in a loving and respectful way. I knew I could do the job and I wanted to. My background as a nurse perhaps made me more suited for this than my other siblings, but this is not why I took on the responsibility. I did so because I felt obliged by life to taste the sweetness of serving in this way. I didn't enjoy every moment of what I was called to do—like many caretakers I burned out from time to time—but because I had created goals aligned with supporting mom in her last years, months, and minutes of life, I was privileged with an incredible experience of life and love that wouldn't have been otherwise possible. Her last words, spoken to me the day before she died at age 96, were "Thank you." Life simply doesn't get better than that!

Mother Teresa wrote, "We can do no great things, only small things with great love." As artists, our goals may not seem so vital or clear as my example above, or as other seemingly lofty or altruistic goals. Does the goal "clean my palette every day" measure up to "paint 100 paintings" as a sweet obligation? Yes, please, assume that it does! Indeed, small goals may be just as important as large ones, if not more so. Small goals, set and met in the spirit of sweet obligation, create the kind of discipline that leads to mastery and fulfillment over the long term.

***

Habit Number 5 suggests you Use Smart Work Strategies. This implies that you oblige yourself (sweetly) to:

- Focus your intention to do art by setting only one goal. Out of all the options you can imagine creating, which one do you choose to invest with your time, energy, and talent? What are 3 small actions you can take immediately to begin? Then, take the first step.

- Create "Structures for Accountability." Structures for Accountability (SFA) are explicit agreements you make with yourself and others to produce work in a committed, responsible manner. A scheduled exhibit or performance is one kind of SFA; a website, blog, or book in which you work to generate content might also serve. The most effective SFAs have: a) one or more people besides yourself enrolled to serve as part of the accountability; b) obvious benefit to you and others for producing as promised, and c) clearly defined, costly, or otherwise painful consequences if you don't follow through.

- Make it a point to work in series. You'll build momentum while flexing the muscle of your ability to explore and sustain an art idea. You'll surprise yourself with a body of work you might not have known you had in you. "It is precisely from the regret left by the imperfect work that another can be born." (Odilon Redon)

- Spend time with art buddies and/or support groups who are as productive as you are—their company can be inspiring and educational. Corollary: Don't hang out with people or groups who take their work less seriously than you do. Unless they are paying you to do so, their company can lead you to complacency and an inflated sense of accomplishment.

- Complete incompletions in your work as soon as you can. Sign your paintings, revise your poetry, show, publish or perform your work sooner rather than later.

- Support your work with good food, exercise, and quiet time, etc. Remember to attend to your basic needs even when you're immersed in fulfilling your aesthetic ones.

Reflections

You may already have one or more Structures for Accountability in place. What are they and how do they work for you?

Do the people you spend time with support your production of art or do they support your excuses for why you aren't producing? If it's the latter, what keeps you coming back to them for more of what you don't need?

Name one sweet obligation/goal for your art that you're aware of today. What Structure for Accountability could you employ to make it easier for you to accomplish your goal?

Habit #6

Deal with Your Demons

I do not understand myself.... For what I want to do I do not do, but what I hate I do. For what I do is not the good I want to do; no, the evil I do not want to do—this I keep on doing.
~ **Romans 7: 15, 19**

A Deeply Fulfilled Artist recognizes when she is avoiding relationship with her art. She identifies the specific ways she distracts herself. She explores her conscious and unconscious blocks to artistic fulfillment.

The Sixth Habit of Deeply Fulfilled Artists recommends a practice of dealing with your demons. Finding expression in apparently benign diversions or routine responsibilities, our demons seem to cast a sort of spell over us and compel us do the opposite of what we intend. We often feel tormented by their presence in our life and helpless to change their negative influence.

Demonic possession is an antiquated notion. Nonetheless the feeling of being controlled by forces beyond our control persists. Demons aren't actual entities, of course; they're internal processes generated by our mind and fueled by our anxieties. These thoughts create a wall of resistance within us of which we are largely unconscious. This aspect of ourselves, which Carl Jung called the psychological Shadow, tends be projected onto people or situations where we experience them as external to us. These projected "demons" then torment us by controlling our behavior.

Suspect you're under the thumb of a demon when you feel as if you're the victim of a person or circumstance. Artists who feel thwarted in their art-making commonly blame time, money, and/or family responsibilities for their inability to work. When these and myriad other factors seem to conspire against you, however, you're probably up against the demon of your own resistance.

Dealing with our projected demons is rarely an easy matter, yet making small efforts along these lines eventually pays off. A simple first step involves making our projections more conscious. By becoming aware of how we participate in a situation, we're often able to find more constructive ways to relate to it.

One way to deal with a demon is to identify the apparent culprit; by giving a name to our internal state we gain some separation from it. I've mentioned that I sometimes overindulge in checking emails or Facebook postings. I've blamed the existence of computers for derailing creative endeavors, sabotaging relationships, and a number of other contemporary ills. Since I started calling this habit my Internet Addiction, however, I've been able to see more clearly that modern technology is not to blame for my plight—it's how *I* use my computer as a time-waster that's a problem. I still occasionally succumb to this and other art-avoidance strategies, but when I do it's with more awareness of my participation in the matter. I no longer feel victimized by the widespread use of computers and the changes they've brought about in almost everyone's lives.[14]

Another level of dealing with demons involves the practice of taking responsibility for frustrating situations in which we find ourselves. The practice is this: Each time you hear yourself say, "I can't," change the sentence to "I won't." For example, are you convinced a tight living space makes it impossible for you to do your artwork? You probably have some internal dialogue with yourself about this or perhaps you'll even catch yourself

---

[14] When the opposing force seems to take the form of an individual, I try to understand that the person represents some part of me and give a name to that.

complaining to a friend that you've tried *everything* and simply *can't* concentrate in your current situation.

Your moment to turn this around comes when you hear yourself utter the words "I can't." Instead of "I *can't* concentrate in my home, try on "I *won't* concentrate in my home." When you change your statement to "I won't," you may be able to connect with that part of you that is so hopeless, disappointed, and angry about the situation that it refuses to even try to find a way for the circumstance to work. If you can feel the negative emotions associated with your choice (and especially if you don't act out of them), you're moving in the direction of taking responsibility for your unfulfilled needs.

Let's be clear that it's only one part of you—not all of you—that attempts to block the desires of your whole self. The "I" that is the subject of "I can't" and "I won't" is your negative lower self-ego. Referring back to the memory of the hurt of some unmet basic need from your early childhood, it continues to defend against feeling the pain it associates with this. And just like the hurt and angry child you once were, this part may act out in some very unlovable ways with the effect of making it difficult for you to get your current needs met.

At bottom, however, the lower self's attempts to prevent your fulfillment are self-limiting. When more conscious parts of you allow the ego the space to declare its resistance outright, it actually starts moving the energy that's been tied up in defending itself. It stops fighting so hard for the right to be negative and relaxes. Once this happens, you'll find it's more possible to declare: "I am willing to find a creative way to work with the space limitations in my home," and actually do it.

Don't expect to cast out your lower self-demons all at once. Pat yourself on the back every time you see how they operate in specific situations in your life. Breathe a sigh of relief when you can occasionally shift from projecting blame to taking more responsibility for your experience. If this doesn't happen for a while and you continue to feel thwarted in your attempts to meet your aesthetic needs, you may choose to seek help from someone trained to uncover unconscious dynamics.

In the meanwhile, ask yourself if there's some way to use your struggle with personal demons to further your art. Henri Matisse once said that he made his paintings in order to understand himself. Bring your struggle to deal with your demons into your art and watch it deepen profoundly.

***

Habit # 6 suggests that you Deal with Your Demons. Begin this process by identifying the distractions in your life. Naming each of them will help you see more clearly how they block your artistic fulfillment. Watch your art life flourish as you withdraw the power you've given to them.

- Name that demon: Identify the nature of what blocks you. Here's a partial list of demons. Feel free to add your own:

Facebook	low self-esteem
alcohol	feelings of overwhelm
time limitations	food
depression	illness
television	procrastination
anxiety	fatigue
market conditions	doubts
laziness	demands of others
fear of rejection	self-criticism
Internet	perfectionism
money concerns	low energy
apathy	shyness

- Identify what distracts you most frequently: Television, email, Facebook, family, dysfunctional people, worry, food, alcohol?

- Manage your blocks and distractions with whatever it takes: Behavioral contracts, books, journaling, support group/individuals, meditation, affirmations, and visualization can be effective tools for helping you refocus on your artistic vocation.

- Get professional help: If your self-help efforts don't seem to do the trick with your resistance, investigate working with a counselor or therapist. Off and on since age 19, I've received tremendous benefit from professional facilitation. People complain about the cost of therapy and, yes, it is expensive.[15] Yet, when you're committed to your life, the value of working through your resistance is usually worth whatever it takes. I've found the methods of Core Energetics and Pathwork to be especially well suited to my emerging Artist.

---

[15] I've never had health insurance coverage for therapy; however, I was determined to get to the bottom of my various dysfunctions and, over 30 or so years, devoted a large percentage of my very modest income to getting the help I needed. I have been repaid not only in personal happiness, but also in being able to value my work appropriately so I earn a decent living.

Reflections

Resistance to doing your art may have its roots in the common tendency to sabotage fulfillment because deprivation is a familiar way of being.

If some of your basic needs were not met when you were a child, you may have developed the habit of denying your needs. Unsure that your needs will be met, you defend against feeling needy. As a result, you become accustomed to deprivation. Believing that this is just "the way things are," you have perhaps become expert at settling for less than what you really require for fulfillment. By re-creating your childhood situation, you unconsciously perpetuate a sense of family, albeit one in which you stay wounded, small, and ineffective.

The unconscious "wounded child" or "lower self," a manifestation of ego, actually resists our conscious self's attempts to change our lives in any significant way and may actually thrive on the negative pleasure it gets from being deprived. The creative energy bound up in this unhealed aspect of ourselves is recovered as we observe and release the pattern of self-denial.

How does your resistance to fulfilling your aesthetic needs show up in your life? Hint: Look for where you tend to settle for less in your life and make excuses to yourself or others for doing so.

What Structure(s) for Accountability might help you become aware of and deal with your resistance?

Are you willing to employ a Structure for Accountability? Why or why not?

Habit #7

Trust the Process

Oh, the places you'll go!
~Dr. Seuss

> A Deeply Fulfilled Artist trusts that the value of her art lies in the making of it. She follows her intuition to discover new depths and artistic possibilities. She finds her life infused with the light of art ideas and gives thanks.

The Seventh Habit of Deeply Fulfilled Artists invites us to value our artistic efforts in terms of the process rather than the product. While we (and others) may prize the result of our art-making, our aesthetic needs are met not so much from holding a finished product in our hands as from creating it.

Fulfillment results not from the repetition of effects deemed successful by the world, but from the exploration, discovery, and innovation along roads less traveled. The deeply fulfilled artist sets aside traditional notions of success and, as a disciple of her process, she follows intuitive inclinations like a divining rod that unfailingly leads her to the depths of the creative well.

It might happen like this:

One moment Karen is baking Christmas cookies, the next she's writing the outline for a new story. Who could have anticipated the six-month dry spell would end in this way? And, had she not opened the laptop and started typing, it might not have. But she did and now central casting has sent a battalion of characters marching front and center onto the stage of, not only a story, but a novel. And, wait, there's more—there's not just one baby in there but triplets. Not just a year's worth of writing, but an epic novel, a life's work, perhaps.

Or like this:

Derek is an everyday painter. He produces one small still life a day, posts it on eBay for a $100, sells ten or fifteen a month—enough to buy supplies, take the occasional plein air workshop, maybe splurge once a year on art camp. Then he loses his day job at the frame shop. The only thing that seems available to him now is night shift at the local convenience store working for minimum wage. He tries it, but is miserable. Tired from not sleeping regular hours, he doesn't feel like he can paint those small paintings any more. Angry, he gets up after a sleepless day and starts throwing paint at a big canvas that's been cowering for ages in a corner of his basement. Without second-guessing himself, he abandons realism. He puts colors together because he wants to, not because he knows they will sell. Hours pass and he's so immersed in the painting, he has forgotten to go to work. "It's okay," he tells himself; for his inner knowing confirms that he needs to keep going in this direction.

Derek waits a few months to begin showing his new body of abstract work, but when he does there's interest. His first Open Studio attracts people who are comfortable paying at least $1000 for a small painting and a lot more for the larger ones he is now producing. But most important, Derek has found his soul in abstraction. Each day he plunges into the unknown using shapes, colors and textures to explore his inner landscape. He gets lost in the work—he's in love.

Habit #7 invites you to trust the process of living your life as an artist. It sounds cliché, but when you're living life at the level of art, it's not the destination but the journey that really matters. The destination—your final breath—is the same as everyone else's. What's different is what you consecrate yourself to along the way. When you really give yourself to your art, you may not know where you're going until you start or know how you're going to get there until you're on the way. As you learn to value your process, you'll begin to trust that the path unfolding before you is leading you where you need to be. You'll find yourself resisting life less and embracing more possibilities than you'd otherwise have imagined.

The goal setting that's recommended by Habit # 5 would seem to indicate that you should know where you're going—how else will you know you've arrived? The Seventh Habit, however, suggests a paradox. It's true that setting goals can be a smart work strategy—goals will surely help you structure a workday. However, attaching yourself to those goals—defining yourself by whether or not you achieve them—may actually inhibit you from attaining the fulfillment you long for.

Your artistic process includes yet transcends the accomplishment of any specific goals. As artists we obtain satisfaction as we allow our aesthetic needs to be met through making art. If we try to force this, however, fulfillment eludes us. Your willingness to make art creates an inner environment in which you want to do art and, with this permission, so you do. It's as if art has a flowing life of its own: We are a part of that life but not in charge of it—we flower to the extent that we enter its flow.

Theodore Roethke, in his poem "Waking" wrote, "I wake to sleep and take my waking slow ... I learn by going where I need to go." Our days on earth are limited. We wake up each day to the reality that we are ever closer to our ultimate breath, to the "sleep" that awaits us. Questions of afterlife aside, the happiness of fulfillment is only possible when we cherish the moment we have presently got hold of. Will the last breath you draw be one of gratitude for a life well lived one day at a time? Or will it be one of regret for roads not taken, a life not lived? It all depends on the value you place upon your life today.

When you come to appreciate and trust the journey as much as or more than the destination, you'll find that where you end up matters less than the process by which you get there. If each day you're fully engaged in the going (i.e. doing your art!) you'll always be content to be where you are—right here, right now—up to and including your last moments of earthly existence. Your own last words will make even your final breath an act of creation.

Let's Get Metaphysical

So far in this book we've discussed the artistic process in your individual experience. Each of the seven habits invites you to acknowledge your purpose as an artist to fulfill your aesthetic needs. They show you how to do this by creating intention and goals, by making the art that you want to make, and by confronting the obstacles that you meet on your path of fulfillment. Finally, they encourage you to value the path of art making upon which you tread as the very stuff of which your life is made. So far, it's pretty much been all about you.

There's another level of art process, however, that's about something more than your individual experience. It's not different from your art path—it certainly includes it—yet it also transcends it. I'm referring here to art ideas and how they come into existence. Some would argue that ideas are simply thoughts generated by the brain. Smart brains produce intelligent ideas. Artistic brains produce pretty ideas. And so on. But what if ideas come before brains?

The Greek philosopher Plato was perhaps the first to suggest that ideas have an existence of their own. We perceive ideas, not because we generate them, but because our brains are equipped with the apparatus to connect with them. Charles Fillmore, a 20th century metaphysician, proposed that our intuitive faculties put us in direct contact with creative ideas that seek expression in the physical world. According to this view, we humans serve as vehicles by which invisible ideas manifest. If we lend our hands, hearts, and minds to ideas, we help bring them to fruition; if we don't, ideas will find someone else for the job. One way or the other, ideas find a way to express themselves.

In the early 90s I met Harry, a man who told me an illuminating story about this phenomenon. It seems he woke up one morning with an idea for a weed-trimming machine. He saw it clearly: A stiff plastic string attached to a lightweight motor would allow the operator to work close to trees, fences, and other places hard to reach by a lawnmower. By his own account, Harry dilly-dallied over this idea. He made some drawings, built a prototype for himself, but never got around to getting a patent. Then one day, glancing through the newspaper, he saw an advertisement for a Weed Eater. George Ballas of Houston, Texas had conceived the same idea. You can imagine how he kicked himself! Still, the experience convinced Harry (and me) that the time for this idea had come—it was ready even if he wasn't and it found George, who was willing and able to take the ball and run with it.

Isn't it possible that art ideas occur to artists in a similar manner? The history of art is a brilliant accounting of how art ideas have broken through into the consciousness of individual artists. When the idea has been powerful enough, new genres have emerged and art has evolved. Perhaps every artist has a shot at being the one through whom these art ideas express themselves. Unfortunately, many of our beliefs limit our availability to serve evolution in this way. For, if like Harry, we don't get around to entertaining the ideas that visit us, they seem to take themselves somewhere more welcoming. (How often I've surfed the Internet and found images I could have painted! I wonder how much my envy of other artists comes of not having followed through on good ideas?)

Imagine yourself waking up one morning from a dream in which you see how to depict light on a landscape by putting strokes of complementary colors side by side. Then, hear the voice of your inner critic chide you for such a silly notion. "Do that and you'll be the laughingstock of the Salon," it warns you. "Do that and you'll never sell another picture." And so you don't. Your buddy, Claude Monet, has a similar dream, however; but instead of giving in to his qualms, he goes to his easel and starts painting. His need to create art matches up squarely with the art idea (Impressionism) to make him a willing and available artist. In your case, however, the need to belong trumped your need to make art. Will you now make misery for yourself and Monet? Or will you take your envy of his innovation as a spur to deal with the demons that keep you playing small, safe, and for the approval of others?

***

The Seventh Habit of Deeply Fulfilled Artists entreats you to Trust Your Process as one who not only perceives your own aesthetic needs and seeks to meet them, but who is also open to giving expression to those evolving art ideas that are seeking fulfillment through you. This implies that you:

- Assess how you appreciate your art process by looking at how you value your art product. Artists who undervalue their efforts tend to minimize the value of their artwork. In a self-defeating vicious circle, the underpriced art is not valued by the buyer either. Look around any Goodwill store to see original art "discards."

- Aim to make the best art you can. As you appreciate an art idea that's seeking expression through you, you will tend to aim higher than if you do with your art what's already been done. Notice if you aim low, creating art that is sentimental or kitschy, or if you're working at the edge of your comfort zone, aiming for a more profound kind of art.

- Honor whatever art you create. Some artists treat their completed creations like hot potatoes. They want them out of their sight as soon as possible so they can get on with the next work of art. For some, this means stuffed in a closet, for others, given away to a friend or family member, or sold to the lowest bidder. It's normal to detach from a completed piece of work, but hiding it or rejecting it may be a sign that you're overly invested in the process end of things.

  Honoring what you've created demonstrates that you value the continuum of your artistic process from conception of the idea, expression of the idea in your medium, and finally through to delivering to the world the idea you've helped to manifest.

- Consider yourself employed by the Universe. A common myth hails the dedicated but starving artist: A *real* artist is the one who forgoes all creature comforts in service to art. Not necessarily! The artist who doesn't eat enough won't be making art for very long. On the other hand, it is helpful to realize that when we serve art ideas, we are compensated for our efforts from their invisible, abundant source. We may not be paid for individual works in the manner we're expecting, but we will be supported. Our part is to do the art and value what we do appropriately.

- Publish your progress. Let the world know about yourself and what you are creating. You'll tend to get more out of your art life when you share your process and product or performance with others. Think of art as a communication from the Great Unseen Generator of art ideas. As an artist, performer, musician, poet, or whatever you are, you position yourself to receive these ideas and translate them into unique forms. You will fulfill your aesthetic needs to the extent that you do this. To be *deeply* fulfilled, however, you'll need to take the step of broadcasting your art to others, thus completing the communication circuit. This task may daunt you and in reaction you may be tempted to either overdo your marketing efforts or avoid them altogether. Work with this temptation. Consider that the world will naturally become curious about your extraordinary life such that sharing yourself will become equally as natural.

So, trust your process and stop hiding your light under a bushel! Keep making art and letting people know about it in as many small and large ways that you can. Bring the painting you've been working on to a critique. Show your dance moves to the director of the local dance company. Submit your poem to the contest. Send a press release to the newspaper. Get in the habit of letting the world know what you're up to. For more ideas, see Appendix 1, "Letting Your Light Shine."

Reflections

Art history mainly records what occurs when artists forgo familiar methods and, instead, trust the process of their artistic expression. Yet, experimentation sometimes threatens our basic need for safety, security, and belongingness; as a result, we tend to seek out what is familiar to us.

How do you play it safe with your art?

What constitutes "good" art for you?

What art ideas do you censor?

What does "aim higher with your artistic expression" mean to you?

PART THREE

SOUL-FULL

Life as a Deeply Fulfilled Artist

If you ... follow your bliss, you put yourself on a kind of track
that has been there all the while waiting for you,
and the life you ought to be living is the one you are living....
I say, follow your bliss and don't be afraid, and doors will open
where you didn't know they were going to be.
~ **Joseph Campbell**

What happens when you become more deeply fulfilled as an artist? How is your life likely to be different than it is today? Will it be worth it to make the changes this handbook suggests?

When I was in my 20s, I suffered terribly from a sense of the absurdity of existence; I could barely envision a future for myself. I believed it would be my destiny to write the Great American Tragic Novel and die at a young age. Only when my father took his own life did I begin to consider that a life could have meaning. I very much wanted to find out why I was alive; in fact, my search for meaning became an overriding passion.

At this time, I was equally preoccupied with finding a husband. I believed that my fulfillment would only be found in a relationship with someone else. I didn't realize then that it was up to me to create meaning out of a deeper relationship with myself. Looking back, I find it interesting that all the while I was questing for meaning and a mate, I would periodically bump into that other guy, Art.

When I was a baby hippie in Roswell, Georgia, I lived next door to Susan Starr, a well-respected fiber artist. I fell in love with the colors she dyed her wool and the rugs and wall hangings she made intrigued me. Her whole life revolved around her art, and I envied her sense of purpose. I asked her to show me some off-loom techniques and, eventually, bought my own floor loom, dyed my own yarn, made my own rugs and wall hangings. Weaving was a hobby, one I practiced for seven or eight years, but abandoned completely when I made plans to attend seminary. And there were the life drawing classes I took for an entire year at the University of Montana in the early 80s. Before I started painting in 2003, I'd do the odd sketch, doodle, or design, nothing I took seriously.

In retrospect I see that I had other needs to meet before I could devote myself to fulfilling aesthetic needs. I believe, however, that art had been waiting patiently in the wings while I prepared myself emotionally and spiritually. Therapy helped me identify what had been missing in my childhood and showed me how to heal from those wounds and the ones I continued to recreate as an adult. I learned how to support myself, both emotionally and financially. I overcame much of the shame and low self-esteem that had held me back from accepting and loving myself. I did finally meet my mate and enter into a healthy marriage. Whew! What a lot of work!

And, wait, there's more!

I started painting in June 2003, at age 52, after careers as both a Registered Nurse and Ordained Unity Minister. For the year and a half prior to that I'd been acting as an advocate for a group of women who, along with me, had been molested by a Catholic priest 40 years before. As part of this effort, I went public with my story in local Atlanta media, which drew national attention. (The New York Times interviewed me!) I went on to participate in meetings in Dallas and other cities with the Survivors Network of Those Abused by Priests (SNAP).

This was a dark period in my life. Not only did the memories of my own abuse resurface, but I was also subjected to the refusal of the local Catholic hierarchy to admit any responsibility for what had happened to to my classmates and me. Once during this time several of us attended an alumni Mass at my old parochial school where the abuse had taken place. After the service, when I tried to introduce myself to the school principal, he turned away and called the police. Such indignities, as well as hearing the stories of the many other survivors with whom I came into contact, left me feeling quite bleak.

As if in answer to some unspoken prayer, I began to experience the presence of a benign feminine spirit that I called The Queen of Happiness & Beauty. When the intensity of what was being uncovered about the clergy sexual abuse seemed too much to bear, I'd go out into my garden and summon her. Under her influence, I was able to perceive a softer, gentler reality than the one I was confronting. I'd try to absorb some of the sweetness she represented and carry it into the next round of battle with the Catholic Church.

In the autumn of 2002, while still wrestling to negotiate a fair settlement with the religious order to which the offending priest belonged, I traveled to Boston for a SNAP organizational meeting. There I found myself unable to sleep for three nights running. Instead, I seemed to hear an inner voice. "Do art," it said. Again and again, this emphatic mantra repeated itself. "Do Art, Do ART, DO ART!"

I returned home from the SNAP meeting realizing I'd more to give to life than what I could for this movement. My new job was to Do Art. I had no idea what sort of art to do, but I recalled where I'd left off at the University of Montana, in a beginning oil painting class that I'd dropped halfway through the term. I bought an easel and basic painting equipment. I assembled the easel and it sat in a corner for more than six months. One day, looking out the window, I caught sight of some blue asters growing in the garden alongside some orange tiger lilies. I ran outside, grabbed a bunch and stuck them in a small pitcher, got out the paints, and made my first painting.

Within six months I'd completed about 50 paintings. Every morning I scrambled out of bed to the easel to see what I'd done the day before. I was thrilled to be learning so much simply by painting each day. It seemed I'd never want to stop. I often felt as if *I* were The Queen of Happiness & Beauty.

Within a couple of years, however, I began to learn about "thwartons." Thwartons are what I call my demons, those outer manifestations of my inner resistance. They show up in benign forms, such as stuck on paint tube caps or brushes I've "forgotten" to clean, and in more catastrophic ones that, since I've started painting, read like a litany from *Lemony Snicket's "Series of Unfortunate Events."* As much as I've felt frustrated by thwartons, I've also experienced the truth in Nietzsche's statement, "One who has a why to live for can bear with almost any how." Practicing the habits outlined in this handbook, helps me recognize my resistance and keep thwartons in their place.

When I began this book on New Year's Eve, 2011, it was from a place of a relatively deep artistic fulfillment, despite two years of living in cramped quarters while renovating a house that would soon be home. I wasn't comfortable, but I was very satisfied with the year that had just completed:

My work had been selected to appear on two popular posters—one for Sleeping Bear Dunes National Lakeshore, the other for our small city, Frankfort, Michigan. I had been awarded a two-week residency through the Glen Arbor Art Association, which gave me time and space to explore new uses of oil paint. I'd given myself the gift of a Master Class with Stuart Shils, a very accomplished artist.

I'd also begun to mentor other artists, integrating my expertise from another career into my present one, and sold more work than ever, in the midst of a down turned economy. Most important, however, was my realization that, as I'd committed more fully to my art-making, my other miseries seemed to subside. I started to see that when I put myself in service to the work of making art, art was giving back to me one hundredfold.

The result has been a feeling of tremendous freedom. I was surprised recently when my work, typically representational landscape, took a turn in the direction of abstraction. I'm really enjoying this expressive work. I love using color so directly, with reference only to the inner landscape. Two months prior I hadn't had a clue this was right around the corner!

Standing now on the brink of what has already been accomplished, I look forward with a sense of possibility and curiosity: I trust that I am indeed going where I need to go. Much of my need to fix or rescue others seems to have relaxed. Instead, I've come to realize (most of the time) that others are guided exactly to and through the experiences they need to get their own needs met. I need only do the Art that is mine to do.

Of course, that's often easier said than done. Life constantly challenges me with unexpected turns and bad moods. As I write today, I've just returned from my winter painting location and moved into the newly completed renovation. Scattered throughout the house are boxes spilling over with stuff I haven't seen for two years. My husband and I both have terrible colds. The buzz of our carpenter's saw grates in the background. And I have a printer's deadline to meet.

Would I be writing this if it weren't for the Structure for Accountability I created to help me complete this book? Probably not. I don't feel like writing today. I don't feel particularly inspired. Yet, as I write, I am aware that something in me believes that I can and should communicate my experience to you, my reader. I notice I am beginning to feel more energized and purposeful. I am not merely "a feverish, selfish little clod of ailments and grievances complaining that the world will not devote itself to making [me] happy." Perhaps by the end of the day I may perhaps experience the part of me that is a "force of nature." Regardless, in this moment, I know I am doing my job, my real job, of creating this book, of fulfilling my need to create my art.

Your *Life as a Deeply Fulfilled Artist*

You're the only one who can decide whether or not you have a future as a deeply fulfilled artist. Your answers to these questions may help: Have you identified with what this book says about aesthetic needs? Are these needs coming into your awareness more and more? Do you feel a spiritual longing to make art?

If your answer is no, then it's likely your primary need right now may be something other than art-making. Living as a committed artist is hard work with little recognition and few external rewards. Unless you're truly called to do more, don't worry about it. Have fun strumming your guitar, singing in the church choir, or dabbling with paints.

If, however, you've recognized that your longing points to a profound aesthetic need, then whether or not you are deeply fulfilled as an artist depends upon making art. The Seven Habits of Deeply Fulfilled Artists can help you to orient your daily life around art-making. They can support you in overcoming entrenched ways of being that thwart your commitment to artistic expression.

I won't promise that if you integrate the habits outlined here you will live happily and contentedly ever after. After all, this is not a fairy tale—it's the infinitely more interesting, creative process that is your life! I can attest, however, that following the call to "Do Art" did eventually bring me into the middle of Joseph Campbell's "field of bliss." If you do your art, I suspect that one day we may meet each other there.

Your Art Life Manifesto

At the conclusion of my Goal Setting for Artists workshop I ask participants to write themselves a letter. The letter is to contain a statement of intent about Doing Art, a few specific goals and any insights obtained in the course of the 3-hour event. Each one seals the letter in a self-addressed envelope and hands it over to me. I hold onto to these important missives until my intuition prompts me to mail them. The letters invariably arrive back in their authors' hands at exactly the right time to remind them of their need to "Do Art."

Why the reminder? Our commitment to listen deeply, to give ourselves what we need most, to do our art, to set intentions, use smart work strategies, deal with our demons, and trust the process ebbs and flows. Everything's great while we're riding the incoming waves but when the tide rolls out, all may seem covered with muck and weeds. At such times, the part of us that's aware of why we must keep practicing can encourage us like no one else. When we remind ourselves of our artistic purpose, we literally renew, refresh, and recharge our connection to our soul, our whole evolving Self.

As you've now reached the conclusion of this book, I suggest you declare in writing what you now believe about yourself as an artist and the practice of art. Many visual artists are accustomed to writing an Artist Statement to summarize the intent of their work; statements like this are published in exhibit catalogues and artist websites. The manifesto I'm suggesting you write at this time is *not* for publication, however. It's for your eyes alone, a reminder whenever you need one.

To this end I invite you to write down the highest thoughts you can imagine for yourself about you and your art. Include your aims and aspirations, your most tender emotions, your most brilliant ideas, specific goals, your philosophy of art-making, what you'd want the artist you most respect to advise you in those times you need a boost, and whatever else you'd like to be reminded of when you're feeling out of touch with your needs and artistic purpose.

Let your writing be spontaneous. Make it a prayer or poem, a litany of affirmation, a love story. Print it out and decorate it. Tape it to the bathroom mirror. Hide copies in secret places. Read it as often as you want. Memorize and recite it. The point is to nourish yourself from the source of inspiration within you.

I wrote such a manifesto years ago and titled it: "The Truth about Me as an Artist." I found it recently when searching for something I'd lost in a stack of papers on my desk in Puerto Rico. The sheet was creased, tattered, and spotted with paint; I hadn't seen it for over a year. I was in a rather frantic state when I discovered the page, yet reading it had the immediate effect of calming me. At first I didn't even recognize the writing as my own, but soon the sentences reawakened me to the truth they contained. I heartily recommend the exercise! It's a great way to support and love the artist you are becoming—your future evolving self.

In the Introduction to this book, I quoted the simple advice: "Let love win." I trust you realize now that letting love win is not only about your relationships to the people in your life. Letting love win is Life's invitation to you to love your whole self and nurture the development that marks its unfolding. I pray the Seven Habits of Deeply Fulfilled Artists will assist you on your path to the next level of your deep fulfillment:

May you listen deeply.
May you give yourself what you need most.
May you do your art.
May you set clear intentions for your art life.
May you use smart work strategies.
May you deal with your demons.
May you trust the process to lead you to your field of bliss.

Appendix 1

Letting Your Light Shine

The notion of self-broadcasting may challenge you in a number of ways that make you think it more trouble than it's worth. Ill-timed exposures, unwarranted or harsh scolding, or other shame-inducing experiences may have conditioned you to hold yourself back from contributing fully to life. You may fear being seen as a shameless self-promoter when you feel like just the opposite.

For example, if you're like many people, you may suffer from what's often called the #1 Fear—public speaking or some other form of stage fright. Perhaps you forgot your lines in the school play or froze up when it was your turn in the spelling bee. Or, as happened to me, a frustrated artist criticized you in an unskillful way. You may have unconsciously vowed never to allow yourself to become vulnerable to such humiliation ever again. You may live that vow today as a false modesty about your successes. You may actually talk yourself out of even recognizing that you have created something worth tooting your horn about.

Today I am not known for shyness; still, I have my ways of withholding. For example, the laptop computer on which I'm writing this contains the mostly finished contents of several books, which comprise hundreds of pages of writing. I love to write and I've been told I'm a natural and good writer. Why then do I have only one book (plus this one) in print today?

I could list a zillion reasons that I've not published more. All of them echo the voice of my mother from a point in the distant past. "Just who do you think you are, young lady?" I can hear it as clearly as if it had been yesterday. And I have absolutely no idea what she was referring to! I'd obviously done something that she considered inappropriate, but I cannot for the life of me tell you what it was. But I can tell you that the tone of her voice has, on more than one occasion, kept me from saying what needed to be said, publishing what I've written, and otherwise doing what was mine to do. She didn't keep me from these things—I allowed myself to be daunted by her opinion of me. No more! (See Habit #6.)

Today I make it a practice to share my art life, in large and small ways, every day, as best I can in the face of those unconscious impulses to hold back. The more I practice this habit, the more it reinforces my legitimacy as an artist, first, in my own eyes, then, in the eyes of others.

Many of my broadcasting efforts are simple and, once I've set them up, automatic. This makes it possible for me to promote my art almost effortlessly. As a result I am recognized and taken seriously in my art-making in the communities where I live and work and beyond. People I haven't previously met, when they greet me, literally exclaim (with some amount of excitement, I might add), "Ellie Harold—the *Artist*?!" Let me say that becoming a celebrity was the last thing on my mind when I started making art. But I see how, when I exist in other people's world as an artist, it means something to them. Because of this meaning, I believe have a responsibility to take myself and my artwork seriously.

What if I just pooh-poohed other's enthusiasm about my work? What if I told them, "Oh, I just dabble." Or, "Yeah, if only I had some talent?" Unfortunately, that's exactly what I hear a lot of the time from very capable artists. If you're one of those who tosses off compliments about your work, or—worse—doesn't show your art to anyone or perform publicly, or otherwise keeps her light under a bushel, consider that you're depriving your audience from something *they* need.

Following is a list of simple ways you can let your light shine. Google or another search engine can provide you with more detailed information about all of these methods:

Business cards A business card shows people that you are serious about your art. It's a great icebreaker with people you don't know. Whenever I meet people, I give them my card. Because it bears the image of one of my paintings, my new acquaintance immediately connects me with my art. If they like what they see, they usually say so which can be very affirming. As a bonus, it often happens that if you offer someone your card, they will offer you one of theirs! (This comes in very handy when creating your mailing list.)

Many online discount printers offer business cards for free or at a very low cost. They provide design templates that you can easily customize with images of your work, quotes, and other art-related content, in addition to your contact information. A business card can be updated frequently without a lot of damage to your wallet. The more you update, the more you'll be thinking about what to include on your card and how you can use it.

Computer Over the years I've learned how to have my public relations work as effortlessly as possible. I don't know what I'd do without my laptop computer. I am not very tech savvy, however, and I'm very grateful for my husband who is. If you don't have a computer, you would do well to invest in one. You may need to take a class to learn about it and/or bribe a friend, neighbor, or grandchild to show you what you need to know to use it. If my 89-year-old Aunt Mary Brent (who never learned to drive) can operate a computer, you probably can too.

Website A website is your online business card—it shows people you are not only serious about your art, but that you're willing for the world to know it. Visual artists have the advantage of being able to display their work, but musicians and writers can post their work on a website as well. Many web-hosting services exist with templates easy enough for non-tech savvy artists to use. Mine is Fine Art Studio Online. For a very reasonable monthly fee, FASO provides me with almost all the public relations and marketing tools I need.

YourName.com Make sure you reserve a domain name for your website that is www.YourName.com. If that is not available, choose something as close to your name as possible. People will remember your name and expect to be able to find you by using it. Your website address (domain name) should appear on your business card and on any other piece of publicity you use.

Email signature You can create a personalized email signature that goes out with every communication you make. I include an image of my recent work, my phone number, website address, and an invitation to view my work. I make it the same size as a business card—it functions in the same way.

Blog Some artists have become quite well known through their blogs. You probably could too if you're willing to learn how to use search engine optimization (SEO) and other Internet tools. I don't blog to gain recognition by the masses, however. I use blogging primarily to help me get clear about my art life and my art works. It's perfectly legitimate to inspire yourself about who you are by reading what you've written. Because it's posted on my website, anyone visiting my site can learn more about me by reading my blog. Be kind to yourself and your readers by staying honest and true.

Social media USE WITH CAUTION. Facebook is a great way to practice making a contribution. Use "status updates" to inspire and uplift people and watch the "Likes" mount up. Posting your observations and insights may seem like a great way to publish your progress; however, keep in mind that this is a fleeting form of publication. Facebook mainly reaches only those people who happen to log on while your post is visible. (Photos, however, do remain in a gallery for others to see.)

Bottom line: Keep making art and letting people know about it in as many small and large ways that you can. Make it a habit to use these simple tools and you'll feel a lot more comfortable with the notion of having a public presence as an artist. You'll get a sense of the way sharing yourself flows into people wanting to support your efforts. You'll begin to enjoy the deeper fulfillment of being an artist in the world.

Appendix 2

(Partial) Art Legacy of C.L. Harold

Created by the children of Charles Louis Harold

Figure Study, Brent Harold, 12" x 11," ink/paper, 1978

Painted Wordless

To spend all my days dreaming up names
for those chips of color: say for shades of gray,
cloudburst, smoke signal, silver lining; for green, *sierra pine
or key lime*
sitting around with a team, perhaps a bit stoned,
tossing out *poppy lipstick, tangerine blush, mellow yellow,
plum crazy*
until the room simmers in a pigment stew.
I always thought I'd be good at a job like that

until today when driving home from Stop and Shop
the forever-leaden sky cracked open
and suddenly the whole world was sprayed copper
shot with rays of rose and pearly gold,
the naked trees, the wandering dog, the cop in the rear view,
my hands on the steering wheel. I almost lost control,
fumbling to name the color of rapture.

~ Beeby Harold Pearson

Free Life, Robert Harold, 36" x 24,"acrylic/canvas, c. 1989.

Bibliography and Suggested Reading

Richard Bach, *Illusions: The Adventures of a Reluctant Messiah*, 1977, Dell/Random House.

Julia Cameron, *The Artist's Way*, 1992, Penguin.

Viktor Frankl, *Man's Search for Meaning*, 1959, Beacon Press.

Eric Maisel, *The Van Gogh's Blues: The Creative Person's Path Through Depression*, 2002, New World Library.

David Bayles, Ted Orland, *Art & Fear: Observations on the Perils (and Rewards) of Artmaking*, 1994, Capra Press.

M. Scott Peck, M.D., *The Road Less Traveled*, 1978, Touchstone/Simon & Schuster.

Joseph Campbell, *Pathways to Bliss: Mythology and Personal Transformation*, 2004, New World Library.

Jill Badonsky, *The Nine Modern Day Muses (and a Bodyguard)*, 2007, iUniverse Books.

Jack D. Flam, *Matisse on Art*, 1995, (Documents of 20th Century Art).

Eva Pierrakos, *The Pathwork of Self-Transformation*, 1990, Bantam.

Maud Morgan, *Maud's Journey: A Life from Art*, 1995, New Earth Publications.

Abraham Maslow, *Toward a Psychology of Being*, 1968, Van Nostrand Reinhold

Acknowledgements

From the beginning, my husband Roo Davison has supported my efforts to make art. Most recently, he encouraged me to follow my muse to Michigan on the painting trip that resulted in the spontaneous purchase of a foreclosed-upon house he saw only in photographs I emailed to him. He then spent more than two years working on this, our new home and my new studio. His faith in my art process holds me accountable in ways I cannot enumerate and for this I am most grateful.

My brothers, Brent and Robert, and my sisters, Beeby and Polly, have each in their own way, at different times, given much to my art life—stimulating environments, rich conversations, hysterical laughter as well as painful disagreements, all of which have highlighted the fun of being from a dysfunctional family.

A connection with a particular place has been vital for my painting. I'm very thankful to the communities of Vieques, Puerto Rico; Frankfort, Michigan; and, especially, Sleeping Bear Dunes National Lakeshore and the Glen Arbor Art Association for providing residency opportunities.

The number of individuals to whom I feel appreciation for their contribution to my art continues to grow; this is only a very partial list: R.A. Moseley; Eileen and Anthony Civitillo, Siddhia Hutchinson, Julie Gearan, Lillian Corrigan, Lynn Hughes, Valerie Gillett, Timothy Tew, Rosemary Sharp, Armand Cabrera, Jill Badonsky, Anna Mallien, Helen and Dan Lautenbach and everyone who's ever bought a painting.